# Grip

# GRIP

## A Memoir Of Fierce Attractions

### NINA HAMBERG

Route One Press  Half Moon Bay   California   2016

Published by
Route One Press
Half Moon Bay, California, USA

The names and identifying details of some characters in this
book have been changed.

First printed in 2011.

ISBN 978-0-9827547-0-2

Printed in the United States of America.
For information, contact Route One Press
www.routeonepress.com.


Designed by Ann Miller, M2Design. Inc.
Text set in Adobe Caslon Pro.

Cover photograph of Nina Hamberg,
New York City, 1967.

To David

I always expected to have an interesting life,

but I never thought I'd be happy until I met you.

# ACKNOWLEDGEMENTS

This book would never have happened without the continued support of David, my husband, first reader and wise critic. Nor would it exist without the years of feedback and friendship from my writing partner, Robin Meyerowitz, who helped me keep going.

When I wasn't sure how I could afford to get the manuscript ready for production, two angels appeared. Ann Miller of M2 Design read the manuscript, designed the pages and created the cover—putting up with my many iterations with continued grace despite the pressure of preparing to open her new gallery, Stone Tiger. I was also incredibly lucky to have the help of Laurie Lieb, a talented New York editor and my freshmen roommate from college, who meticulously read the manuscript and gave it a professional polish.

My thanks to Mira Miriello for her close reading and even closer friendship, and to Sherry Freimuth and Tina Holland who were sure that what I was doing was worthwhile.

I've been fortunate to be able to work with exceptional writers and teachers whose insight helped me unspool the narrative thread. In particular, my thanks to Janis Cooke Newman, Judy Goldman, Adair Lara, and Diane Higgins Hannan.

And lastly, my deepest appreciation to my amazing mother, who admired every poem I wrote as a child, who believed in me as a writer, and who, the last time I ever saw her, beamed at me when I assured her I was going to finish this book.

– NH

# FAMILY

# I

We gathered around the small kitchen table as though the breach had never happened. The same blue and white checkered cloth covered the Formica top. A stick of margarine lay in the chipped plastic holder next to a saltshaker that was always sticky.

My mother thrust the dishes over to my brother—hot baked potatoes wrapped in aluminum foil, yellowish canned peas, and finally a meatloaf made with Borden's evaporated milk. Then she stepped away from the stove, yanked her chair out and sat down, her lips pinched. My brother took some of everything, even the peas, which he hated, before he slid the plates to my father.

In years past, we'd all be talking by now but tonight no one spoke. My brother poured ketchup over his meatloaf until the edges disappeared. I concentrated on peeling the wrapping off the potato, trying not to make noise. Finally, I glanced over at my brother sitting across from me. His hair was slicked down and swept into an Elvis wave in front, like most other sixteen-year-old boys in 1962. He rolled his eyes.

"What?" I mouthed.

My brother shook his head but didn't speak.

After most of the food was gone, my father turned to me.

"Tell your mother, if she wants to use the car, she better ask me in advance."

His face was red and his voice shook. I'd never seen him angry like this. My father would have made a perfect spy. He was the kind of man who could slip by unnoticed. Doughy and pear-shaped, of average height, with horn-rimmed glasses, thinning brown hair and a soft voice, he was suited to his job as a school librarian. I glanced over at my mother. She looked like Debbie Reynolds in *Singin' in the Rain*, almost five feet tall, just a little bigger than me. She was sitting right there. I peeked back at my father and slouched down.

"Tell her," he ordered.

"Dad says you should ask him when you need the car," I muttered, twisting around so I didn't have to see him.

"You explain to your father that everything we own is half mine, including the car. Tell him I'll take it when I need it." Her back was rigid, her teacher's posture, the stance she used in front of her class.

I swiveled in my chair to face my father. My voice sank lower. "Mother says everything belongs to both of you."

"You inform your mother that she can't dump everything on me, then waltz back in scot-free."

He didn't even bother to glance at me. He was almost spitting out his words, staring straight across the table.

My mother turned to Ron. He looked back at her and blinked, the color disappearing from his face. My brother never got pulled in.

"You tell your father, I'm the one who worked for everything we have. I'm the one who supported this family. I have a right to anything in the house."

Ron stared at his plate and mumbled. It continued that way, my parents using my brother and me like puppets for a few more minutes, until my father shoved himself back from the table and strode toward the den. A moment later, my mother rose stiffly from her chair and marched upstairs, leaving us to clean up the mess.

Three years before, when I was ten, my mother had enrolled

in a graduate psychology program in Miami and took me with her. Ron stayed behind with my father in Queens. We were supposed to be away from New York for one year, but within a few months, from the way she talked, I was afraid we'd never go back. While I was growing up, my parents had never argued. I thought they were happy. But in Florida my mother complained that my father was a miser who recorded every dime he'd spent on their dates. She said he was a weak man who whined about finding a job while she'd slaved away as a substitute teacher in the Bronx slums, her salary holding the family together.

To her, my father was a failure, but that wasn't how I'd seen him. He was the one who carried me to my bed after a long car trip, even though I was only pretending to be asleep. He was the man who could fix anything, who'd unroll a felt pouch with tiny screwdrivers and repair my Cinderella watch while whistling tunes from *Your Hit Parade*. But after hearing my mother's tales of disappointment so many times, her view conquered mine and I felt betrayed by him as well.

During those years in Florida, I saw my father in the summer, sometimes visiting for a month. But at the end of August when I was thirteen, my mother told me I should stay with him and start high school in Queens. She'd remain behind in Florida to finish her doctoral dissertation, then come back to New York in less than a year and make a new life, a better life, for my brother and me.

But she returned much sooner than that.

A lawyer had told her that she needed to occupy the house for a month if she hoped to win it in their divorce settlement. I never knew if she'd consulted my father on her plans, but they surprised me. She showed up one day in late September when the marigolds were still in bloom.

My mother took over Ron's old bedroom in the attic just down the hall from me, sleeping on a twin bed under wallpapered eaves with images of prop planes diving through a night sky. I kept the same pink bedroom I'd had all along, the one my father and uncle had built for me, with a recessed dresser and cubbyholes for my dolls. Downstairs, my father stayed in my parents' bedroom surrounded by the massive mahogany furniture they'd bought when they married. My brother moved into the knotty pine paneled basement my father had finished for Ron's bar mitzvah three years before.

One night, a week after my mother's return, I followed her into the den. It was her turn for the TV room, eight o'clock, time for *Playhouse 90*, an hour-and-a-half live drama that she said was the best show on the air. She settled into the brown vinyl La-Z-Boy chair, lined up directly in front of our thirteen-inch black-and-white screen, while I sat on the daybed in the corner, slouching against the wall. I never liked *Playhouse 90*, but I didn't really care. I was done with my homework and it was something to do.

At nine o'clock, my father appeared in the doorway. He still had on his gray work slacks, but he was wearing just his sleeveless white undershirt, his favorite attire at home, even in winter. He never seemed to notice how fleshy and pink his upper arms were, how exposed he looked.

"Get out. You've had the TV for an hour. Now it's my time," he said to the back of the recliner, his voice high and tight.

"I'm not ready," my mother said from the other side. "There's another half hour to go."

"Get out. My show is coming on."

She shifted her weight in the chair as though she were bolting herself in.

"No. I want to finish this." She stared at the screen.

I knew that *The Phil Silvers Show* was about to start. My father loved comedy and this was his favorite program. He never missed it. Every time Sergeant Bilko, the sly chubby soldier in charge of the motor pool, pretended he didn't know how to play poker my father chuckled. So did I. I'd rather be watching Phil Silvers, too.

He stomped into the middle of the den and stood, feet apart, his hands on his hips.

"Get out now."

"You can't make me," she said, not turning to look at him. It sounded like something an eight-year-old would say.

In a few quick steps he was around behind her, grabbing the top of the La-Z-Boy and pulling it back until my mother was upside down staring up at him.

"Get out of here," he screamed, glaring down at my mother. Then he let the top of the recliner spring from his grip. It snapped upright so fast, I was afraid she might shoot out of the chair and slam into the TV. Without glancing back, he lurched out of the room.

As soon as he'd gone, she leaped up and rushed over to me, kneeling alongside the daybed. "Don't ever leave me alone with him," she said, sounding strained and hoarse, as if she'd been the one shouting.

She reached over and grabbed my hand and although I saw her clutching me, I couldn't feel anything. I nodded, barely breathing. What did that mean? What was I supposed to do? My father weighed two hundred pounds, twice as much as I did. I came up to his chest. How could I defend her? When she dashed out of the room seconds later, I trudged after her through the doorway and upstairs to my room, my legs thick and wooden beneath me.

My parents slid into a standoff after that. They didn't speak to each other, ordering Ron and me to scurry back and forth between them instead. But my brother had friends who drove, so he could get away. I was the one who was trapped.

At the end of October, my mother told me she needed to return to Miami by herself so she could finally finish her dissertation. I wasn't sure if this was the real reason, but since I'd already started high school, it made sense for me to stay. In some ways, I welcomed her decision. My father was easy to get along with when she wasn't around. He did the cooking, the cleaning, the laundry, all the chores I'd been assigned in Florida. And he was home much more than my mother ever was. He was predictable and reliable. With him, I wasn't as lonely.

So, four weeks after she'd come back to Queens, my mother carried a stack of her clothes into my room, dumped them on a chair upholstered with green and pink tulips, pulled her dinged-up blue suitcase out of my closet and opened it on my bed. She began folding her clothes quickly, a nylon blouse with pearl buttons, a Madras plaid skirt. I sat on the bed a few feet away, not talking, just watching her pack. I felt tired and heavy, the way I did most of the time. All I wanted to do was crawl in bed and sleep.

Something crashed below us, followed by the smack of footsteps on the stairs. My mother dropped the blue chiffon scarf in her hands, leaned toward me and whispered in one quick breath, "Don't leave me."

There was no time to reply. An instant later, I heard my father before I saw him, growling. "No, you don't." His voice was torqued, like a twisted towel, so compressed it didn't sound like it could be coming from him.

My mother edged in front of me as he surged into the room. At first I thought she was moving to protect me, but from the angle of her body, I sensed she wanted to underscore my presence, to use me as her shield.

"I won't have it," he said, his feet planted wide apart. "You're not walking out again. You're not leaving me high and dry for another year."

"I have to go back to Florida and finish my doctorate," she said, turning away from me to face him, her voice barely wavering.

"You're not going without giving me my freedom."

"We haven't come to terms yet." She stood up straighter, glaring at him, acting as if they were the same size and she weren't a foot shorter and a hundred pounds lighter.

"You're not doing this again. Do you hear me, you bitch!"

He'd never used that word. It distorted his mouth and then it changed his body. He seemed to grow larger. His face turned scarlet. Then, in a fraction of a second, he charged at my mother and threw her against the wall. Her back hit the plaster with a deep thud, the sound of the first rock crashing in an avalanche. He pinned her by the throat, stiff-armed and leaned into her, his white shirt damp with sweat, his back heaving like he'd run a long way. My mother didn't move, didn't try to resist. Her feet barely touched the floor. She held herself as still as the live butterflies my brother used to pin on a board. My father was unrecognizable, as though his softness had been a disguise, a cloak to hide the truth that underneath the excess weight hid a weapon of a man.

It was all happening so fast. It wasn't real.

He held her there, suspended for an instant before his arms fell limp to his sides and he released her. Neither moved. Then he turned away and as he did, he appeared to shrink, a man who hated to raise his voice, who never swore. It seemed to me he moaned but I don't think he did. The only sound that came from him was the slap of his footsteps going down the stairs, slowly and deliberately, as if he couldn't see where he was heading and had to feel his way to the landing.

My mother's eyes darted around. Her voice raced as she said she was getting out of there, driving over to Judith Cohen's house. She grabbed her purse and sweater before rushing out of my room.

I hadn't budged from the bed where I'd been sitting, next to my mother's open suitcase. I didn't want to get up but I knew I couldn't stay there. I had to go somewhere else, too. But my body felt huge, impossible to move. After what seemed like a long time, I forced myself to rise and lumber downstairs, dragging my shoulder against the stairwell, letting the wall hold me up.

At the base of the stairs, I saw my father in the living room, hunched over on the knobby brown chair that he and mother had upholstered together in night class. His shoulders were shaking. His nose was dripping. Tears streaked down his face and he just let them slide off his chin. He gestured for me to come over and I did—I felt I had to—squatting a few feet in front of him.

"I'm so sorry," he said, no longer looking at me.

I stared at him without replying. His face had turned rubbery and wrinkled.

"I'm sorry you had to see that. When you're older, you'll understand." The words bore their way out of him, broken by gasps for air.

His hands were clasped on his lap. He opened them and raised them toward me, but I was out of his reach and I was glad. I didn't want his touch to contaminate me.

He dropped his hands and moaned. A moment passed. He rocked back and forth, slowly at first, then more insistently, like a man in prayer, sobbing and muttering, "When you're older, you'll understand."

I stood up, barely looking at him, still silent. What was I supposed to say? That it was okay, that I understood, when it wasn't and I didn't.

I let the screen door slam behind me. Judith Cohen's house was miles away, farther than I'd ever walked, but I couldn't think of where else to go. I trudged down our block and onto the next, over cracked concrete sidewalks that had buckled where some fault line must have given way. Somewhere a radio announcer called out a baseball score, a bicycle bell jingled. I was crying so much it was hard to breathe.

There were stones in my stomach. I hated my mother. Why couldn't she just give my father a divorce? She didn't love him. Why not tell Ron to protect her? He was older and bigger. Why me? And my father? He'd been a chump. Who wouldn't be mad after all these years? But why did he have to blow up in front of me? Why did I have to watch?

My canvas sneakers had smooth rubber soles, copies of the style rich people wore on sailboats so they wouldn't mar their wooden decks. Usually they were fine for walking, but now they stuck to the pavement, every step an effort. I wanted to smash my parents together, squeeze them into a brittle little ball and hurl them as far away from me as I could.

A year later, more than four years after my mother first left him, my father finally got the divorce he wanted. My mother was awarded her doctorate, the house in Queens, and my brother and me.

# 2

I'd expected my mother to move into the master bedroom once my father left but she never did. She continued to sleep in my brother's little boy's bedroom upstairs. Ron hauled his things from the basement to the den and stretched out in the sagging daybed next to the television. When no one else claimed it, I camped out in my parents' old bedroom, an easy choice. Because it faced the backyard and was private, I could leave the blinds up and feel the sun when I awoke. Like so many things in our family, there hadn't been any discussion about switching, we just claimed other beds. Still, it felt odd—no one where they should be—like we were mismatched playing cards sorted into the wrong decks.

The next summer my mother headed out on a fourteen-day cruise on the *Ile de France*. She was going to do something nice for herself for once, she said. She'd sent Ron and me to summer camp, paid for my dancing lessons, but she'd rarely splurged on herself. So for a few weeks when my brother was eighteen and I was fifteen, we had the house to ourselves. Since we didn't really have anything to do, we decided we'd surprise my mother by refinishing her old bedroom set and making it look like new. It would fit in with the redecorating she'd been doing, part of our fresh start.

One night, after she'd been gone for over a week and hours after my brother and I had plodded off to bed, I was jarred from sleep by a light so intense it felt like morning. I turned my head toward the window and faced a blinding white wall, like the headlights of an oncoming truck.

Someone was standing outside my window in the dark and he wanted me to know he was there. Fear surged through me, as piercing as electric current. Then my thoughts returned.

*What should I do? He wants to see me, to spy on me. Don't let him.*

I reached for the faded blue sheet down by my feet and pulled it over my head. On the other side of the fabric, I could still make out the light, probing, focused and cold. Within an instant, a sharp, slamming sound came from the direction of the window. He must have punched the glass.

"Ron, there's a man outside," I shouted to my brother sleeping in the next room, yelling as loud as I could, wanting the man with the spotlight to hear me.

There was no reply. My brother had always been hard to wake up.

"Ron!" I screamed.

"What? What do you want?"

"There's a Peeping Tom outside my window."

"You're dreaming." His voice was slow and heavy.

"I'm not. He's right out there shining a light on me."

My brother sighed. "You're okay. Go back to sleep."

"Get up and look."

"He's not hurting you. He'll go away." Ron sounded muffled as though he were talking into his pillow.

Outside the beam clicked off.

In the next room, Ron made a grunting sound and then there was silence. I was sure the man was still there waiting for me to uncover myself. I could almost feel his presence. At least now the man knew I wasn't alone. He wouldn't dare do anything with my brother here. I waited. Five minutes went by and sweat matted my pajamas to my skin but I didn't care how hot it was. I'd sleep under the cover all night if I had to.

The glass rattled again, but softly, more plaintively, unlike the previous outraged sound. A moment later a twig snapped in the distance, then a scraping sound. The man was giving up and leaving but I still didn't move. I listened for any clues, feeling my hearing grow as acute as if I'd become a sonar device sweeping the dark yard. Where was he? Was he in the far corner by the Stillers' lawn, holding a pair of binoculars and waiting for me to sit up? I continued to clasp the cover over my face, holding myself very still, afraid any movement would reveal my presence. Finally, when there was no other sound than the crickets and I felt certain he'd gone, I pulled the sheet back, rose and scurried over to lower the blinds.

The next morning, Ron clumped into the kitchen at eleven. I'd already been up for half an hour. When he dressed up, slicked back his hair and took off his glasses, my brother was really handsome. All my friends had crushes on him and I didn't blame them. But now Ron's eyes were puffy, barely open. He plodded across the linoleum floor as though he had webbed feet. His wrinkled plaid shirt was open, showing matted curly brown hair covering his arms and chest, even climbing over the top of his shoulders. He had on the same shorts he'd worn all week, and he smelled like a dog just out of its kennel.

"Come on. Let's go check the backyard," I said.

"Hang on." Ron held up one hand. "I need some fuel," he said, filling a bowl with Kellogg's Frosted Flakes.

I pushed him from behind.

"We need to inspect."

"What's the big deal? You don't need me to look. Go yourself," he said, pouring milk over his cereal.

"I want to do it together." I grabbed his arm.

"Take it easy. This is going to spill." He slurped up some cereal, grinned, then followed me, carrying the bowl with him.

There were footprints of a man's shoes in the dirt right under the back window, alongside the zinnias. In one place, the heel had left a deep imprint.

"See, I told you someone was here." I felt triumphant that there was such irrefutable proof and moved a few feet back to let Ron get a closer look.

"Hey, I believed you last night," he said, squatting over the impressions.

"What should we do?"

Ron straightened up. "Nothing. You probably scared him away. He won't be back. Anyway, these guys are harmless."

My brother shrugged his shoulders and smiled. He braced his cereal bowl against his chest with one hand and, with the other, clasped my neck from behind, a gesture that allowed him to maneuver me like a rider controlling the reins. Usually I hated when he did this and I would swat away his hand, but now I was just happy for the contact.

"So what do you say, squirt? You going to obsess about this all day or are we going to finish the dresser?"

Just before Ron started walking and steering me forward he seemed to pause. I was sure I knew what was coming next, one of the snide remarks he used to goad me. I half expected him to say that the Peeping Tom must have been blind, because I was too flat-chested to bother with, the same way he'd joked that if I went to the beach in the new topless bathing suit that had been making headlines, no one would notice. But he didn't. He just angled me toward the side door and ambled along beside me. Even though we never called my father or anyone else, even though nothing happened, it felt as though something good had.

By the end of the two weeks, Ron and I had taken my mother's twenty-five-year-old mahogany highboy, dresser and night stands down to their original surface, stripped off the dark finish, sanded the wood, then wiped on a natural stain to give the set a contemporary look. The furniture came out so well we congratulated each other. But later, when my mother gasped at their flat, slightly pinkish color, I realized we'd ruined them.

It wasn't the only attempt at updating the house that failed. Earlier that spring, as part of her new approach to life, my mother decided to replace the living room furniture. I was delighted to get rid of the 1940s teal velvet armchairs and the coffee table with spindly legs, symbols of my parents' failed marriage. I remember the particular triumph I felt seeing the faded pink damask couch with a fringe that looked like the corkscrew curls in a Victorian matron's hair exiled to the curb, waiting for the garbage truck.

The style my mother and I selected was called Danish Modern, the name alone exciting. We ended up furnishing our living room with a royal blue couch flanked by a pair of hanging brass lamps that looked like something from a Middle Eastern bazaar. Our new side chairs were covered in the same burlap as the couch, but in a yellowish green that the salesman had assured us was the year's hottest color. Our rose-colored wool wall-to-wall carpeting was replaced with a dark blue nylon one that seemed to draw dust. Within a few months, it was clear that these pieces made our house feel cheap and flimsy. The stodgy old furnishings had been indestructible; these felt like a theatrical set.

Thinking back, maybe the Danish Modern set suited us, because we began talking to each other like characters in a play, holding onto our roles and never going off script. During my high school years, my mother was the hardworking, aggrieved breadwinner, my brother was the sarcastic, primping young fop, and I was the intellectual, condescending teenager. Often, our quips seemed less for each other than for some imagined audience off to the side.

My brother lived at home and commuted to college, but I couldn't wait to get away. The next year, at seventeen, I enrolled at an all-women's school. My freshman year there, my first time separated from my family, was one of the happiest of my life. But when I returned home in the summer of 1966, my hands shook at the dinner table. I couldn't get much food down and lost so much weight, my ribs showed. I obsessed about ending my life. I didn't know what was happening to me and only much later understood how much anger I'd been carrying toward my mother, and what transpires when rage is swallowed whole.

For the most part, I had to deal with that turbulent time by myself. My father had remarried and was focused on his wife and stepsons. My mother had become engaged to a widowed podiatrist from Long Island and spent her days at Sidney's oversized ranch house trying to win over his two daughters, coming home mainly to sleep. My brother didn't even come back for that. He was finishing his undergraduate courses in summer school and spent weekday nights at Sidney's because it was closer to his college. At least, that was the reason Ron gave but I think he felt as confined in our home as I did.

By the end of summer, I comforted myself by listening to Bob Dylan's new album, *Blond on Blond*, staring at his out-of-focus face on the cover, imagining he was singing "Sad Eyed Lady of the Lowlands" to me, and counting down the days until I was back at college.

# 3

One night, two weeks before the start of the fall semester, I was downstairs in the bathroom leaning over the pedestal sink, just about to rinse out the Crest, when I heard a loud crash. I froze, gripping the porcelain edge with one hand, clutching my toothbrush with the other. The noise sounded as if a metal garbage can had been knocked down but it seemed to have come from the dining room, not twenty feet away. There was no one in the house except my mother and me. We'd said good-night to each other fifteen minutes earlier and she'd headed upstairs to bed. I wasn't sure how long I stood motionless at the bathroom sink before I heard another loud crash nearby.

"Call the police. There's someone in the house," I shouted up at the ceiling. Then I caught a glimpse of myself in the mirror. My face was the same chalky color as the toothpaste. I reached over to the bathroom door and locked it.

Minutes later, I heard two taps.

"Mom?"

"Are you okay?" my mother said softly.

I opened the door and peered at her.

"Did you call?"

My mother nodded. She'd been in the middle of setting her hair. Pink plastic curlers covered half of her head, while her hair, flipped up into a wave, bobbed cheerfully on the other.

"You've probably just imagined it," she said, and patted my arm.

No one in our family had ever phoned for the police. I'd

never even seen them on our street in Queens. I'd been afraid that my mother might be too embarrassed to call—maybe bringing in the police was a lower-class thing—or that she wouldn't believe me, given how freaky I'd been all summer.

Ten minutes later my mother answered the doorbell when it rang and led two policemen into the house. They had on dark blue uniforms with brimmed caps like those worn by railroad conductors. Both men were tall, but with handcuffs, guns and clubs dangling off their hips they looked gigantic, barely able to squeeze through the hall. My first impression was of older men, maybe in their thirties or forties, but when one spoke, hooking his thumbs through his belt loops and spreading his legs wide apart, he seemed like a boy playing policeman. I realized he wasn't much older than me.

"I'm Officer O'Malley and this is Officer Puzzo," he said. He took off his cap and wiped his forehead with the back of his hand, revealing hair the color of carrots, flattened on the sides.

His partner snapped his gum, grinned and wrote our names down on a little pad, the kind waitresses used in diners. He was young, too, with an eager energy.

I stepped closer, ready for them to interview me. I'd already thought about how I'd describe the sounds, but before they could ask me a question my mother turned to the red-haired officer.

"You look very familiar. Were you in my biology class at Andrew Jackson?"

She worked as a guidance counselor now out in Long Island and hadn't taught biology in years, but she still ran into old students around the neighborhood.

"No. I went to Sacred Heart. Maybe you had my younger brother," O'Malley said.

"Oh, good. I was afraid I might have flunked you." My

mother chuckled. It was a private laugh, because she knew almost no one failed her class.

I shifted my weight from one foot to the other, feeling as I often did with my mother. She was four feet, eleven inches tall, only an inch shorter than me, but I felt lumbering and huge around her, dark while she was blond, sullen while she shined. Now she was winning the police over and I was starting to disappear.

O'Malley smiled. "If he looked like me and barely squeaked by, it must have been Roger."

"How's he doing?"

"Pretty good. Got one kid. Works for the city sanitation department in the Bronx."

"Please say hello for me, will you?"

I wanted to tell him that I felt certain she had no idea who his brother was.

"Sure. I'll do that. Now, what seems to be the problem?" he asked my mother.

"My daughter thought she heard a noise. Maybe a burglar tried to break in."

My mother chatted confidently. She'd finished setting her hair before they'd arrived and it amazed me now. How could anyone be at ease with a head full of rollers and bobby pins?

"I see. You two the only ones here?" O'Malley asked.

"Yes." She hesitated as if she wanted to say more but didn't.

"Right," O'Malley said. "We'll take a look." Then, turning to his partner, "You go around the back. I'll check the front and sides."

The one chewing gum nodded. He pulled a black flashlight off his belt the way boys yank toy guns from their cowboy holster. I stood next to my mother in the doorway and watched a beam glide over her white Chevy convertible in the driveway.

I hadn't heard any strange sounds since I'd yelled to call the police. Now I was starting to feel the way I did at a doctor's office when the pain disappeared as soon as the physician strode in. The police weren't going to find anything. They'd resent me for wasting their time.

I thought about running after them and telling them to check the flower beds in the backyard for footprints. Maybe the sounds I'd heard came from outside the house and not the dining room at all. But before I could decide what to say, the police were back inside our house.

"No sign of anyone. Nothing broken or disturbed," O'Malley said.

"Listen, I'm sorry if we caused you any trouble," my mother replied.

"Not at all. No problem." He turned to me for the first time. "Most likely you heard a branch snap. Something like that. Everyone's a little jumpy right now after what's happened."

He didn't need to elaborate. The week before, a sniper had climbed up the clock tower at a university in Texas and started shooting the people below, killing thirteen. The story was on all the news shows. And here was the crazy part—he hadn't known the victims. It made no sense.

"Yeah, I guess," I said, slouching.

Why bother pointing out that there weren't any trees close to our house? My mother gave me the same kind of tight smile she used when I was six and knocked over a glass of milk at the dinner table.

"Would you boys like something to eat before you go? I have fresh coffee cake," my mother said.

The one cracking his gum glanced longingly toward the kitchen.

"I've got nice Oreo cookies."

"No, thank you. We've got to get going," O'Malley said, his hand on his partner's sleeve, guiding him toward the front door.

I wanted to tell them to wait. I wasn't imagining those sounds. But I stopped myself because maybe they were right—maybe I had.

# 4

The temperature kept rising for the next six days, the air dense with humidity. New York Augusts were often in the nineties, but this weather felt heavier and less forgiving, rarely easing up after dark.

"Are you going to be able to sleep in this heat? Maybe you should leave your windows open." My mother had come into the master bedroom to say good-night. Now she glanced toward the wall of aluminum blinds, shutting out the backyard and things we hadn't used in years—a barbeque, a picnic table, the shed with a rusted lawn mower and my old English racer.

"No, I'll be fine like this," I said.

Ever since the Peeping Tom, I'd been careful to keep the blinds drawn, and the past week, even though the police hadn't found anything, I wanted the downstairs sealed up.

After my mother padded out, I looked around. It still amazed me that I had this room to myself. It was the place I'd sneak into as a child, sliding the dresser drawers open and peering at my father's black socks, rolled into balls and laid out in straight rows like crops, or my mother's rhinestone pin with two kangaroos unfurling a banner. I investigated every item many times, sensing that these objects—my father's penknife with a green pearl handle and my mother's folded linen handkerchiefs—held the secret to who my parents really were.

My father's possessions had been gone for a long time but my mother still stored some things here. One drawer held her sweaters, entombed in yellowing zippered plastic bags. Another held her collection of 1950s nylon scarves, each one telling a story. One was a travelogue of France with floating blue and green Eiffel Towers, smiling waiters and the word *Paris* in red at angles. Another was a Western scene with cowgirls clasping the reins of a bucking horse with one hand, waving with the other. When I was growing up, my mother had worn them wrapped tight over her head and tied at the back of her neck, like a movie star, like Grace Kelly or Brigitte Bardot. She also had small pastel chiffon scarves, the weight of butterfly netting, that she'd knotted loosely around her throat.

After she went to bed, I peered through her things, through the same clothes I had donned for dress-up as a child. I'm not sure what had made me think of playing belly dancer with her scarves earlier that week, but once it entered my mind, I knew it was a great idea. Just as I'd done for the past few nights, I stripped down to my underwear. Then, shaking out one large scarf after another, I tucked the corners into the top of my underpants and tied the little chiffon scarves to the straps of my bra. Lastly, I fastened a scarf over my nose and mouth hiding most of my face.

I switched on the lamp on the nightstand and turned off the harsh overhead light. The table lamp was one of a matched pair from Germany, with a plump baby angel sitting on a mountain of porcelain flowers, leaning forward, holding a chipped rose. I climbed up onto the bed so I could see myself in both of the gold leaf mirrors that hung over the dressers on opposite walls.

I turned around slowly, feeling the nylon brush against my thighs. I couldn't remember the last time I'd liked looking at myself. I'd gained eighteen pounds the summer I was sixteen, bussing tables at my aunt and uncle's restaurant in North Carolina and eating entire pecan pies at one sitting out of boredom. Despite two years of diets, I hadn't been able to shed the extra weight. Now, after finding it hard to eat since I'd been home from college, I was down to ninety-eight pounds, thinner than I'd ever been. This was the only good part of falling apart. Looking back at me from the mirror was someone I didn't know, a slender woman—veiled, mysterious, desirable.

I held my hands out six inches from each ear, gliding my head from side to side in a movement I'd learned from an Indian dance. I rotated my hips in a slow circle. The fantasy that had come to me fully formed—the same one I'd had for the past several nights—took shape again in my mind.

My mother has been kidnapped by a sheik. She is bound to a wooden chair in the next room, blindfolded and alone. It is up to me to save her, but there is only one way I can do this. I must entertain the sheik. If I stop dancing or if my movements aren't pleasing, his men will kill her.

I stood sideways to the mirror and glided my torso back and forth like a cobra swaying out of its basket. Years of dance training had given me flexibility, but I'd made up this move myself.

"Yes," the sheik said, "this is good." He shifted his position on a dark wooden chair with lion claws carved into the feet.

We were in a large tent with canvas sides. The light filtering in was gauzy and diffuse. The sheik's skin was bronze, his eyes almost black.

My hands circled in toward my chest and the scarves swayed on my legs.

"Such lovely long hair," he said.

I swayed and spun on the bed, trying to think of inventive moves like opening and closing my fingers as though they were fans, but after ten minutes, fatigue seeped into my body and my arms drooped. Even before he spoke, I knew the sheik was angry.

"Is that all you can do?"

He leaned forward in his chair and his robes rustled.

I started swinging my hips in a wide circle like a hula girl, tapping imaginary brass bells with my fingers. The sheik nodded and settled back.

I danced for another few minutes before glancing at the clock on the nightstand and almost losing my footing. It was time to stop. I climbed off the bed and the sheik slowly dissolved, the way the smoke rings my father blew for me when I was little vanished bit by bit.

I folded each scarf into a square, stacking them back in the drawer where I'd found them. I peeled off my underwear. It was so hot I'd probably sleep better without anything on. I glanced at my nightgown draped over the chair. It was the same kind of nylon as the scarves. It might feel cool against my skin. Just before climbing into bed, I slipped it on.

I must been asleep for hours because I was in the deepest sleep, the dreamless state, when I sensed something reeling me in, as though I were a kite slowly pulled down to earth. Gradually, I felt myself in my bed again, under the thin blue sheet. Then I realized I was almost awake. And I wasn't alone.

*Mother?*

All I smelled was the faint scent of bleach rising from the pillowcase, not the Chantilly Lace cologne that coated everything she wore. I waited for her to say something, to call out my name, but the only thing I heard was a soft crumpling, like the sound of tissue paper.

I opened my eyes and saw a shape, an outline with no features, the cutout of someone who wasn't there. My glasses were on the nightstand beyond my reach, and even if I'd had them on, it was too dark to see. The shape glided toward me like a submarine. From the size I could tell it was a man.

It had to be someone I knew playing tricks.

I wanted to close my eyes and slide back into sleep. It felt so close. Then I thought, I might still be asleep and dreaming.

I reached up to wipe a strand of hair from my lip but when it stuck to my skin and pulled, I knew. I was awake. I was awake and there was a shadow in the room.

*Was it my mother's fiancé?* That didn't make sense. Sidney lived thirty miles away. Why would he be in my bedroom? Something must have happened to my mother and he'd come to tell me.

"Sidney?" I said to the empty form.

"Be quiet."

"Are you Sidney?"

"No. Keep quiet and you won't get hurt."

*What other man could it be?* I knew. It had to be my brother, trying to scare me. He'd loved to terrify me when we were kids. Maybe he'd snuck in to frighten me. I wouldn't let him see I was afraid.

"Ron?"

"No. Keep quiet." His voice was louder. The shape grew larger.

"Who are you?"

Silence.

*Dad?* Had my father come back to their bedroom? Why would he do that? He'd remarried years ago and was away on a vacation with his wife. It didn't sound like my father's voice. But he was the only one left.

"Dad?"

"No."

"Who are you?"

This was my home. He had to be someone I knew. If I found out who it was, then everything would be all right. *Think.*

The man loomed over me, pulling back the cover, and I felt a wind cut in. How could the air be this cold against my arms? He lowered himself in one quick move, sitting tight against my side. His weight carved a hole in the mattress.

"Who are you?"

"Just shut up and you won't get hurt."

He smelled like car oil or Vaseline.

I didn't know him.

There was a stranger in the room, on my bed beside me. *What did he want? To kill me? What should I do?* I was suffocating. *Think. What did Ron once tell me? If a man comes at you, poke him in the eyes.* But he didn't teach me how to do it. I sat up halfway and thrust out my hand. My fingers crumbled on either side of his nose just above the lip.

"Don't do that." He sounded amused.

"Okay. I won't." I lay back. I didn't think it would work.

He leaned over my chest and face and the bed cringed. One of his arms formed a stake against my ribs and the other rose to my throat.

"Who are you?"

Silence. I heard him breathing, a pinched, tight noise, and for a moment I thought he was going to tell me.

"It doesn't matter who I am. I know who you are, Ni-na." Slowly, sharply, he spewed out the words, my name so filthy it defiled his mouth.

It was as though he had taken a sledgehammer and shattered my sternum. I broke into splinters. *He knew.* That was why he was here. He'd seen the cold part inside me, the way I'd used people, and he despised me. *No. No, he couldn't have.* I grabbed hold of the pieces. *Don't say that. Stay here,* I thought, snapping myself together. My hands folded over my belly, over my sleeveless nylon gown with blue and green daisies. I clutched the thin slick fabric, glad I wasn't lying here naked, grateful for this little shield.

The man leaned in closer. He gave off the heat of a dog's mouth. I felt something hard and straight against my throat, like the metal edge on a wooden ruler.

"I've got a knife. Shut up or I'll cut you."

I raised my hand toward my neck. *What was this?* It was cold and thick and smooth, but the outside edge was jagged. I felt a row of gaping saw-teeth. This didn't make sense. The back of a blade was straight.

"That isn't a knife."

"Yes, it is." His voice was raw. He increased the pressure until there was heat at my throat, as if he'd lit a cigarette lighter near my skin.

I wanted to merge with the mattress, sink down among the springs and the twisted cords, melt into the wooden slats of the box spring. *This wasn't happening. Think. I must know something. What have I read?* Yes, I remembered. *If a man attacks you and you can't fight him, start talking. He can't do anything if you keep him talking.*

"You don't want to do this," I said softly. "Let's go to the kitchen. We can sit down and talk."

"Shut up or I'll slice your face."

"You don't want to do this. Let's just go to the kitchen. I'll make you a cup of coffee." *What if he said yes?* I didn't know how to fix coffee. *What could I give him? Milk?*

"Shut up. Shut up or I'll cut you in pieces."

He was spitting at me, growling. He was so close. The room smelled like soiled newspaper at the bottom of a cage.

When I spoke again, my voice was faint. "What would your mother say if she could see you now?"

The words surprised me. It didn't sound like anything I'd ever say. I wasn't even aware I'd formed the thought.

A high whine erupted from deep inside his throat. He yanked his hand away from my neck, reached down between my thighs and shoved up my nightgown. His other hand squeezed my breast.

*This wasn't about killing me. He hadn't come to murder me. He was here to rape me.*

My bones hardened across my chest. I could not allow it. If I lay still, I'd be helping him harm me and that would shred my spirit. I knew it with a fierce clear certainty. If he wanted to rape me, he'd have to knock me unconscious or murder me first. I would not cower and submit.

I opened my mouth to call out to my mother to phone the police, to warn her, but the sound that erupted was gigantic, volcanic. Its velocity blasted him back. It flooded the bed, the floor and kept on surging—so much more noise than I'd ever made, a mountain of agonized sound.

The man sat up fast, hesitated for a second, then jerked his hand down like he was yanking on a leash. I felt something heavy and wet. He'd poured oil on the sheets. No, that wasn't it. He scorched my leg. My thigh was on fire and I hadn't stopped screaming.

He leaped up and ran. As he cut through the doorway I saw his outline, saw a shadow slice through the dark and disappear.

I could barely breathe in the silence. The air was a blanket encrusted with soot. I pulled myself up and leaned against the headboard.

From far away I heard my mother call out, "Are you dreaming?"

I had to search for my voice. It was hiding.

"No," I murmured. Then loud and brittle, "Call the police. There's a man in the house. Don't come down."

I wrapped my arms around myself for warmth. It must have been eighty degrees in the room, but my teeth wouldn't stop chattering.

# 5

Several minutes later a light switched on in the hall and I saw my mother framed in the open doorway, the ruffles on her nylon nightgown worn flat from washings, the once pink color stripped to a streaky white. A turquoise paper cap, designed to preserve her bouffant hairdo, swelled around her head.

"Were you having a bad dream?" she asked, stopping a few feet from the foot of the bed.

I stared at her face, glistening with the cold cream that kept her from wrinkling, afraid she hadn't believed me and picked up the phone.

"Did you call the police?" It was hard to say even those few words. My lips were cracked and dry.

"Yes." She hesitated. "Were you having a nightmare?"

It was the same question she'd asked when I was little and she'd woken me gently, sitting beside me and stroking my hair. I raised my left hip to show her the proof, the streaks of blood on the sheet and the slash running down my thigh.

"There was a man in the house. He cut my leg."

Her body teetered for a moment; then she rushed to me, dropping into the same place where the attacker had sat.

"My poor baby," she said, clutching me.

I didn't want to be touched yet. Not by her, not by anyone. The rancid smell of the intruder still filled the room. But it was more than that. I recognized this hug from my mother. It said *love me, reassure me, comfort me.* Maybe I would have responded differently if she'd rested her hand lightly on my arm, but not an embrace like this—not one that wanted to siphon so much out of me. I shrank back, pressed my hands to her shoulders, easing her off me.

"Don't do that right now," I whispered. "Please, leave me alone. I just need to be by myself for a few minutes."

I looked into her face and saw everything soft hardened. I had done the one thing she couldn't bear—I'd pushed her away. Her body stiffened as if I'd struck her and she shot up so quickly, the bed shook. I wanted to chase after her as she turned away, to plead with her not to shut me out, not now when I needed her help. But it was too late. I could barely feel the edges of my own body. The blood was starting to thicken on my leg, but I had failed her. I'd withheld my affection. Now she was the one who was injured, not me.

As soon as she left the room, I started to shake. I wrapped my arms around my torso, pressing myself together so I wouldn't rattle apart.

It seemed like a long time passed, but it was probably only ten minutes before the doorbell rang and I heard my mother walking down the hall. Not her usual quick pace. Instead, her steps were slow and cautious, the way an old person moved when they fear they might fall.

I didn't want the police to find me in bed. I rolled over on my side, carefully easing my nightgown away from my thigh. I looked at my leg. A crust of blood had sealed over the gash. It was still weeping in one place, but otherwise the wound had almost stopped bleeding. I forced myself to stand.

"My daughter's in the bedroom over here," I heard my mother say.

She entered the room first, a cotton housecoat over her nightgown, the paper cap gone from her head. Behind her were two policemen. I'd expected to see the same young cops who'd been here the week before, but these men were old and worn. The face on one was puffy, his dark shirt straining across his belly, every pocket stuffed. The other one held a clipboard. His glasses looked like the pair my father wore, sturdy, boxy, out of fashion.

"A man broke into the house and attacked my daughter with a knife," my mother said, her voice thin and stretched.

"Who else is here?" the heavy policeman said.

"Just my daughter and me."

"Where's your husband?" the one with the clipboard asked.

"We're divorced."

He clicked the top of his ballpoint pen twice with his thumb.

"No men in the house?"

"I have a twenty-one-year-old son. He's staying at my fiancé's."

Then my mother hunched down and looked away. I'd never seen her disappear like this.

The policemen waited. Finally the one with the clipboard turned to me. "Well, what happened?"

I tried to tell him but my voice was so low, he had to ask me to speak up. I began again, staring at his shoes. They were thick, black traps at the end of his legs.

"Sounds like an unhappy boyfriend," he said when I'd finished.

At first I couldn't make sense of his words. They were so stupid.

"I don't have a boyfriend."

"Maybe a former boyfriend then," the fat one said.

I'd barely dated in high school.

"I don't know anyone who would do this."

The heavy cop paused and squeezed his eyes shut. A pained

expression crossed his face.

"Was it a black man?" he asked, opening his eyes, straightening up and inhaling deeply as though he could smell the black man in the room.

The cop with the clipboard looked at me kindly and nodded his head up and down, signaling yes.

*Was it?*

"I don't think so. No."

The heavy one sighed, then spoke to his partner. "Maybe it's the same guy from St. Albans."

St. Albans was a black community ten miles away. They turned to my mother as if I were no longer there.

"A black guy's been breaking in and attacking colored girls there all month," the fat policeman said. Almost to himself, he added, "But this guy doesn't use a knife."

"Yeah. He's always shown up early before, about 10:00 p.m." his partner added.

I looked from one to the other. This made no sense. I waited for my mother to point out the inconsistencies. She had a quick mind and a Phi Beta Kappa key, but now she stared past the policemen, silent and rigid. Only her hands moved, burrowing inside the pockets of her housecoat, as though she were searching for something trapped in the seams.

"It doesn't sound like the same man," I said finally.

The cop with the clipboard lifted the top sheet and read something on the page beneath it. His partner scratched his palm, then his nose, then studied the ceiling. I realized they were ready to leave. They hadn't written anything down or gone outside to see how the intruder broke in, but they were done here.

I moved a step toward them and forced my voice to be strong.

"Shouldn't you go look for him?"

Neither responded. Then the one with the clipboard said, "What would we charge him with?"

What would they charge him with? I'd watched Perry Mason reruns after school for years. I knew what had happened was illegal.

"How about breaking and entry! What about assault with a deadly weapon!"

They both glanced down.

The chubby one said softly, "He's armed."

I was having trouble standing. My leg was pounding. Maybe the cut had reopened. I wanted to lie down and hide under the covers.

"You've got a gun!" I pointed to the weapon strapped in his holster.

"All right. Don't get excited." The heavy cop held up his hand like he was stopping traffic. "We'll check it out. Okay?"

He nodded to his partner and they scurried out the door.

After their engine started, I waited for the squeal of their tires, the whine of their siren, but all I heard was a car slowly driving away. They weren't going to hunt for the attacker. They weren't even pretending to try.

# 6

M ary Kramer, our next-door neighbor, opened her door moments after my mother pressed the buzzer at three a.m., saying the commotion had already awakened her. Mary was a small woman, the same size as my mother and me, but plump and hard.

When I was a child, I'd knocked on her door many times, always with a good reason. My mother was still at work and I was hungry. A big splinter had lodged in my palm and had to be removed. My brother was supposed to be watching me, but he'd darkened the house and turned on *Shock Theater* to scare me. Mary stared at me like I was a stain on her carpet, never wanting to let me in, but I'd learned that if I stood in front of her, looked hopeful and waited, she'd give me what I wanted. She complained to my mother that I was a little manipulator and, with Mary, I probably was. But she was always home and I didn't know where else to go.

Now Mary gestured for us to follow her inside, her expression wary but resigned. I slipped in behind my mother, watching the slouch of her shoulders as we walked down the hall.

"A man broke into our house and attacked Nina with a knife. We called the police," my mother said, her words rushing into one long string.

"I knew something must have happened. I heard a car peel away a half hour ago. It must have parked on the corner outside my window. I saw the cops arrive," Mary said.

My mother reached out and tapped Mary's back. Her friend glanced around.

"Can we sleep here tonight?" my mother asked softly.

"Of course, Bunny."

Mary switched on the fluorescent light and led us to her kitchen table. She hadn't greeted me or even acknowledged I was there. The room was infused with a yellow light but I could feel the darkness pressing in around us. I slid into the seat against the wall. My mother sat on one side, Mary lowered herself across from me. No one spoke. The only sound was Mary's nails, tapping against her Formica top, brisk and persistent, as though relaying a message in code.

Mary finally turned to my mother. "Bunny, you want to call Sidney or Ron? You're welcome to use the phone."

My mother had slumped down in her chair but now she jerked up, her voice tinged with anger. "What can they do now anyway?" She sighed, weary again, and said, "There's no reason to frighten them in the middle of the night. Tomorrow is good enough."

Mary rose, filled her whistling tea kettle and, when it squealed, poured the hot water into three cups, over bags of Lipton tea. My mother reached for her mug and grasped it between both hands, the way she did in winter when she clutched her cup for warmth. My tea sat a foot in front of me, brown and foreign. I thought I should take a sip but my arms didn't want to lift from my sides. Every part of me was going numb. Even the throbbing in my leg receded.

Mary reached over and patted my mother's hand. I'd never seen Mary touch anyone with affection, not her big, slow son or her husband, who sliced animal pelts for a living. My mother squeezed her eyes shut and tightened her lips and for a second I thought she was going to cry. But she didn't. She never did.

"Why did this have to happen?" my mother said.

Mary made a tiny shrug with her shoulders. Then she glared

at me, her black eyes narrowing, flashing disgust. She was mad at me for upsetting my mother.

I realized I could no longer feel the back of the vinyl chair. I was starting to disappear. Mary's clock above the refrigerator had always made me smile. It looked like Felix the cartoon cat, with its flicking tail, its gaze pivoting from side to side. But now the tail whipped back and forth, the eyes were bulging and crazed. I had to get out of this room.

I leaned toward my mother and whispered, "Can I go to bed now?" surprised I could still speak, that anyone could hear me.

She nodded and reached down for her purse.

"It may be hard for you to fall asleep. Take this," she said, opening her bag and handing me one of her Librium sleeping pills.

After I swallowed it, the three of us rose. Mary led us down her hall, stopping to pull a set of faded floral sheets and an assortment of linens out of her closet.

"We can make up the sofa, Mary. You've done enough already," my mother said once we'd walked into the den.

Mary nodded. "I'll wait for you in the kitchen." She shot me another angry look.

My mother flipped on the table lamp, then stood at one side of the knobby gold couch while I went to the other. We pulled open the sleeper sofa and as soon as we'd made up the bed I climbed in, aware I was finally lying down but unable to feel the sheets.

"I'll be back in a little while. I'm going to go sit with Mary," my mother said, turning off the light.

The mattress sagged beneath me and the sofa's upholstered back coughed out dust but I was too leaden to care. I'd just closed my eyes, welcoming the sensation of drifting away, when my hand brushed against my stomach and felt the slippery texture of nylon. In an instant, I was awake. My throat seized shut. *Was I still wearing the same nightgown?* I couldn't remember; then I recalled I had changed back in our house. This one was fresh and unharmed. I started to breathe again.

I had almost drifted off again when I heard my mother's voice, fierce and sharp, rising from the kitchen. "What kind of daughter does that, Mary? You tell me. What kind of daughter pushes her own mother away?"

The next morning I didn't want to open my eyes when my mother shook my shoulder, saying, "Come on, Nina. We can't stay here all day. We're in Mary's way."

"What time is it?"

"It's after ten."

My mouth was so dry it was hard to talk. "I don't want to go back to our house."

"We have to." Her voice softened. "It will be all right."

My mother led the way across the driveway and I followed her into our kitchen. Everything in the house seemed blurry and distorted, as though I'd opened my eyes underwater.

"Stay here," she said as we stood by the stove. "You don't have to go into the other rooms, not ever again."

"What about my things?"

"I'll bring them out to you," she said.

A weight lifted from me. I didn't want to see the damage in the bedroom—the sheets would be seared, the carpet scorched.

I lowered myself into a kitchen chair and watched my mother tense up, thrust out her chin and stride into the den where my brother usually slept, the room adjacent to the master bedroom.

"The screen is on the floor. The man must have pushed it off. There's a big fingerprint on the wall where he pulled himself in." She called out each discovery. There was a pause; then she added, "It looks like he shoved the picnic bench underneath the window to climb in."

I saw each of the things she described as clearly as if I'd been standing beside her. I thought I'd closed and locked all the windows, but I must have forgotten the den. Moments later she came back into the kitchen and dialed a number on our black wall phone, pressing the handset tightly against her ear.

"Sid?... Oh, Ron, it's you. Listen. An intruder broke into the house last night and attacked your sister."

I stared at my mother, hoping to track information on her face, but she turned her back to me. For years, I'd been waiting for Ron to stand up for me. He never had, but so what. This was the time that mattered. He was twenty-one. He worked out with barbells. Now he would come to my defense.

I heard my mother say, "Ah huh. No. I don't think so. What time did Sid say he'd be back? Okay. Be sure to tell him. Yes, we'll be ready."

She hooked the handset back on the receiver with effort.

"What did Ron say when you told him?"

My mother paused, pinched her lips together, and looked down at the floor.

"He wanted to know if the man touched his coin collection."

I pictured my brother, his hair carefully sculpted back, his hands in his back pockets, his lips curled in a smirk, and a surge of anger flared in my chest, focused and hot. But within moments it extinguished. I didn't have the strength to keep it going.

Time dissolved as my mother moved through different rooms. I heard a crash as she pulled a suitcase from a shelf. Later, she slid into a chair next to me and put her hand on my arm. The blue in her eyes seemed paler. The color was fading.

"I think we should get you to a doctor. Someone should look at your leg."

Her words felt like a slap, jarring me awake.

"No!"

"You should get a tetanus shot."

"I don't need it," I snapped. The thought of anyone probing the cut was unbearable.

My mother let go of my arm, sighed, stood and walked to the sink, lifting a cup out of the dish rack. She wasn't going to fight me.

By noon, it was too hot and humid to remain in the kitchen so I slipped outside, sitting on the front stoop of our house, pressing my knees together and resting my head on top of them. The air felt heavy. I pretended it was a cloak that could hide me.

It was a Saturday, and up and down our street men were easing their Oldsmobiles out of their driveways, pushing their lawnmowers across their grass, moving their sprinklers to the middle of their yards. These were men I'd known most of my life, and the attacker could be any one of them. He could be on the block right now, waiting.

Five houses away, Pete the mailman yanked at the strap on his worn leather pouch, hanging from his shoulder and bulging with letters. He'd delivered our mail since I was four and every Christmas my parents gave him a crisp ten-dollar bill to thank him for his service. He looked the way he always had, the same blue-gray uniform, but now I realized he was wearing lace-up black shoes, the kind with rubber soles. He could have crept into my house without my hearing him.

I watched him stuff envelopes through a mail-slot a few doors down. Pete the mailman knew every house. Was he the one?

A bell jingled in the distance and I watched as Uncle Bob turned the Bungalow Bar Ice Cream truck around our corner. I could make him out through the windshield, cruising the street, one hand on the wheel, the other tugging the cord that rang the bells, a confident look on his face. This was his territory, not the Good Humor Man's. When I was young, he'd let all the kids pay for a popsicle the next day if we didn't have enough change. But he'd gasped when I returned from Florida after being gone for so long, a thirteen-year-old in a padded bra, no longer the scrawny kid he remembered. At the time, I thought he was shocked that the years had passed so fast, but maybe that wasn't what he was thinking at all.

I watched as he pulled to the curb in front of two waiting children, bounding out of the truck, jogging to the side, opening a refrigerator door and reaching into the cavity so far that his arm vanished in the white smoke of dry ice. Uncle Bob knew all our names. Was he the one?

A door slammed nearby. Wallace Kramer, Mary's son, with waxy streaks on the lenses of his glasses, lumbered out of their house next door. He was only five years older than I was but he moved like an arthritic old man. Wallace sat in his room all day and stared at the walls, and when he came out, he apologized: sorry for brushing against the back of a chair, for dropping a spoon and making a noise, for needing a soda when his mother was fixing a roast. He will later be sent to Creedmore, a huge, desolate, state-run hospital for the insane, and when he returns home he will hang himself.

Wallace Kramer was too big for the shadow I saw running out. He couldn't be the one. Could he?

Suddenly, all the noises of the street, the intermittent hiss of garden hoses and the grind of tires on asphalt, dimmed.

Instead I heard an inner voice, sharp and certain. *No man can be trusted.*

# 7

I couldn't stay outside. It was too exposed. By two in the afternoon I was huddled back in our kitchen when my mother's fiancé, Sid Ross, steered his black Cadillac to the curb in front of our house. He honked his horn several times before shutting off the gas and getting out to help us carry the suitcases and old beach bags that my mother had crammed with our things and lined up in the front hall. Sidney was a big man with a bulbous nose who called himself The King, often ducking under doorways when his head would have cleared.

There were three men who could have helped me then: my brother, my father and my mother's fiancé. I hardly saw Ron the week I stayed at Sidney's house even though he was there, too. I slept a good part of the day, sharing the bedroom with Sidney's sullen twelve-year-old daughter, barely waking up when she rooted through her closet for clothes in the morning or at night when she snored. But it wasn't just a difference in schedules that prevented Ron and me from talking. My brother utilized the same skill he'd honed as an adolescent—he made himself scarce.

There were no conversations with my father that week either, at least none that referred to the attack. He and his wife were back from their car trip to the Pennsylvania Dutch Country and I'm sure he must have chatted with me on the phone, describing the horse-drawn carriages, the heavy German food, the colorful hex signs on the barns. But I'm improvising this now because I cannot recall any of our exchanges before I went back to college. I can only guess that the absence of what I longed to hear—his concern, his outrage, his desire to hunt the bastard down and hurt him—left such a hole that all my father's surface talk vanished in that crater.

The only one who said anything about the attack was Sidney. The next morning, on Sunday, when I made my way into his kitchen, hungry for the first time, he was standing next to my mother, leaning over the counter, munching on a toasted English muffin. I was wearing shorts and a T-shirt and when I was some fifteen feet away, my mother called out for me to stop and turn around. I did, moving slowly. He glanced over, took another bite of his muffin and told my mother her worries were misplaced, the cut was nothing, no need for me to see a doctor or get a tetanus shot. I had two feelings in quick succession—relief the cut wasn't going to be probed, and despair. Sidney had two daughters but he wasn't going to stand up for me.

A week later, when the fall semester started, I was glad to be back at college and away from my family. The first afternoon had been set aside for orientation, and all the students were expected to attend. By the time I wandered over to the Student Center, it was already filled with hundreds of buzzing girls and a handful of eager boys who'd probably raced over from the nearby men's college. I scanned the faces, looking for my closest friends from my freshman year, but I couldn't find Laurie, my former roommate who'd short-sheeted my bed, or Sue, who played late-night gin rummy with me until our thumbs wouldn't bend, or Nadine, the first girl I knew to give a boy a blow job.

I braced myself against the back wall and watched as girls in the lounge paired up, talked for a few minutes, then regrouped. There was so much motion that, at first, it looked like they were amassing signatures for their high school yearbooks, but after a few minutes I realized they were collecting something else. Stories. These buoyant girls, in blouses with bright swirling flowers and paisleys, were seeking out anyone they recognized and asking "How was your summer?"

One reply after another drifted back to me.

"I stayed in Jersey and worked at my dad's hardware store."

"I went to England with my folks."

"I was a counselor with bratty eight-year-olds at the shore."

"I made up a biology class at summer school."

"I hung around the house and drove my mother crazy."

A girl from my old dorm stopped in front of me. I couldn't remember her name. Her brown hair was free and gentle on her shoulders. She smelled green like Irish Spring soap.

"How'd your summer go?" she asked, cocking her head slightly to one side, smiling.

*What should I tell her?*

A rush of images blurred in my mind, then there was no thought at all. Like someone in a trance, I raised my plaid kilt skirt a few inches and angled my leg out toward her. A red snake of a scar now slithered down the back of my thigh. In just a week's time, the scab had been replaced with dense, ropey skin that had wrapped itself over the incision as if it couldn't protect the wound enough.

I was surprised to hear my own voice, as lifeless as a zombie's in a horror film.

"I was attacked. A man cut me with a knife."

The girl didn't move. Her mouth jutted open but no sound came out. She took several steps back, still facing me, before she turned and rushed away.

A skinny boy strolled over wearing tight levis, a striped red-and-white T-shirt and a black wool sports coat. He had curly dark hair that rose a foot from his head, framing his face like a fuzzy halo. I remembered him now, Paul something. I'd met him at a fraternity party Nadine dragged me to last year. He was a drug dealer who sold high-quality LSD and grass.

"Hey," he said. His lips curved upward just enough to convey a greeting.

"I was attacked."

I lifted my skirt and twisted my leg so the back of my thigh faced him.

"See," I said in the same flat voice.

He gasped. His eyes darted around, looking for the fastest route away from me.

I didn't move. A girl from my freshman English class glided over to me. Then another. Every time, I showed them the scar.

I sought out more people, prowling the floor of that churning room and stopping girls I barely recognized. Each one stared, then fled and I couldn't blame them. I would have done the same thing if some freak approached me like that. I didn't know why I felt driven to expose myself, not realizing how hungry I was for someone, anyone, to express outrage over what had happened. After showing the wound many times that first week, the compulsion to reveal it closed over. In its place, a fantasy began to obsess me, flickering in the space between dreaming and imagining.

I am in the bedroom in Queens, wearing my sleeveless nylon nightgown. It's the same night the attacker broke in. The heat, the darkness, the silence, everything is exactly as it was with one exception. This time, I know he is coming. I see myself hiding behind the open bedroom door, clasping a cast-iron skillet with both hands, ready. As the intruder creeps in, staring at the decoy I've created with my pillows under the sheet, I leap out, wallop him in the back of the head and knock him unconscious. I am elated. My plan is working!

The scene changes to the kitchen. I've dragged him in there and bound him to one of the chairs with clothesline. I'm standing over him, seething, waiting until he opens his eyes. Unlike in real life, I see what the attacker looks like. He's bony and small. His short-sleeve shirt hangs over a sunken chest. He has thinning, greasy brown hair and fingers stained from nicotine. Finally, his eyelids flicker and he comes to, disoriented. As he glances at the striped wallpaper on our kitchen wall, then up at me, his mouth opens with surprise. He tenses, squirms, trying to twist loose, but within seconds, his body goes slack. He's trapped and he knows it.

This is the moment I've been waiting for. But before I can confront him, opaque tears skid down his checks and drip off his chin.

"I'm sorry. I didn't mean to hurt you," he whimpers in a paper-thin voice.

This is so unexpected that, for an instant, I don't know how to respond. Finally I yell, "You had no right!"

"I never meant to harm you. Please, let me go." His words come out in ragged gasps.

I feel swollen with anger but I can't rail at him because he has become so pitiful. All I can manage to say is "You frightened me."

More tears seep from his eyes and his shoulders shake.

"I'm so sorry. Please. Just let me go."

I don't want to release him. He should be punished for what he's done. He could harm someone else. But he has become so weak, I don't feel I have a right to hold him.

I untie the knots and set him free.

This fantasy tracked me down almost every day, in many places. It found me when I was alone, curled up on the sofa in the silent dorm living room writing poems after midnight or stretched out on a knoll staring at the sky instead of struggling to stay conscious in French class. Each time, it was largely the same but there was always some difference—like footage for a film in which a scene is shot over and over because the actors can't get it right.

In another version, I'm lying in my parents' bed, exactly where I was when the intruder broke in, but this time I'm not asleep. I'm just pretending. Hiding in the corners of the room are big strong teenage boys who've come to help me. They are unlike anyone I'd ever known, the kind of boys who'd stop a bully if he picked on their sister. When the attacker creeps in, they jump him and pummel him until he blacks out. They drag him into the kitchen and bind him to a chair with rope. Thinking their job done, the boys saunter out before the man comes to. Then the attacker wakes up and starts to sob.

In every fantasy, his voice is watery and high, not like the sound of the intruder in real life, but still, so familiar. He whimpers that he couldn't help himself, he never meant to harm me. He pleads with me to release him. I want to shout at him, "What you did was wrong." I want to shake him until he rattles apart and I get justice, but I don't. He seems so desperate and frail, more wounded than I am, that once he begins to beg, I can't stop myself. I release him.

I disappeared into versions of this daydream for weeks but it made no sense. The attacker hadn't collapsed when I'd confronted him, he'd become more terrifying. I only knew one man who'd sobbed like that—my father. Somehow the different episodes of violence in my home had fused together so tightly I couldn't pry them apart. No matter how many times I struggled to hold onto the image of the real intruder in my daydream, I failed. Once I'd captured him and tied him up, his voice became my father's, beseeching me to help him—just the way he had the summer I was eleven.

When we were first planning our move to Miami, my mother assured me we'd return after she'd obtained her master's degree. We did come back to Queens a year later, making the two-day train trip and sleeping upright in the coach section, but my mother had no intention of staying. She'd brought only one suitcase and had our return tickets in her orange clutch purse. I don't know what my parents said to each other about the future, but my father seemed willing to pretend everything was all right the week we were there.

On our last night home, I found him in their master bedroom. He was staring out the window at the backyard as I came into the room. It was almost bedtime and we hadn't even said good night.

"Daddy?"

He turned to face me and gave me a faint smile.

"That's a pretty blouse. Have I seen it before?"

"I wore it yesterday."

"Oh, I wasn't sure."

He took a few steps over to the highboy. On top was the wooden box that held his personal things, the box no one else was allowed to touch. He lifted the lid, removing the green pen-knife he'd owned since he was an Eagle Scout, turning it over in his hands, before setting it down. He removed a pocket watch, then a tiny notebook, putting each back carefully, lining them up. I'd seen him straightening out his things like this before but why was he fussing with his little treasures now? We were leaving in the morning and I wouldn't see him for another year. There was almost no time left and so much needed to happen.

I wanted to tell him all the things I'd promised my mother I wouldn't: how she'd started going to dances wearing her white sheath dress and the earrings that looked like bird cages, how I was supposed to call her by her first name now that she had a boyfriend who flinched when he saw me. I wanted to tell my father he was the only one who could make it better. He had a workshop in the basement. He repaired the toaster, wristwatches, the TV, anything that was broken. He could fix our family. I wanted to shake him and shout he had to stop pretending he didn't know how. But I couldn't yell at him. He seemed as soft and porous as cotton candy.

He closed the lid on his box and asked, "Where's your mother?" His voice sounded tired and sore.

"Next door, at Mary Kramer's house. She went to say good-bye."

He walked over to the bed and lowered himself down on their blue chenille spread. The sides of his mouth drooped. His eyes were almost closed. I didn't know what to say. I went over and sat next to him. I saw us in the mirror, a heavy man in a pressed short-sleeve shirt, a small girl with a pony tail, sitting side by side, like people on a train.

Suddenly, my father jerked his chin toward the backyard and stiffened. "You know, it's the one thing I ask your brother to do. Mow the grass. That and take out the trash. Look at it. He's fourteen. You think he'd lift a finger!"

Suddenly all the sharpness left him. He pulled in his breath and, squeezing his eyes shut, emitted a sound I'd never heard him make, a low wail. He pinched his face tight, the same way I did when I didn't want to cry, but tears forced their way out of his closed eyes.

*I could mow the grass for him.* Then I realized it couldn't be the lawn. *Had I done something wrong?*

"Daddy?"

He started to say something, but stopped. His face reddened

but he still didn't look at me.

"Daddy?" I touched his arm. He was frightening me.

Huge tears washed down his checks, so many, so fast.

Then my father whispered, "Don't leave me."

"What?" I wasn't sure I'd heard him.

"Don't go." He started to sway back and forth. "I've been so lonely."

I felt a pressure gathering in my chest. *What had I done?*

"You don't know. I've missed you so much," he said.

He pulled me to him and I wrapped my arms around him as best I could. As he cried, his smells leaked out, the sweet sticky scent of aftershave, the oily aroma of hair cream, the biting odor of deodorant—everything was washing out of him. My father was dissolving and I had to hold him together.

"I'm so sorry, Daddy." I started to sob, too.

"So many nights coming home to an empty house. Don't go," he moaned.

I hung onto him. I'd make it all better. "I won't leave, Daddy."

All year, I'd been furious with him for abandoning me, for letting my mother take us away, for never coming to Florida to visit. Now it seemed I had it all backward. I was the one who'd deserted him.

Later that evening when I informed my mother of my decision to stay, she shook her head and replied, as dispassionately as a judge, that a young girl belonged with her mother. She was returning to Miami to get her doctorate and I was going with her. No matter how much I pleaded, she didn't waver. I was relieved she'd made the decision for me because I didn't want to choose between them.

That fall semester at college, I wore sunglasses indoors, blackened my eyes with liner and mascara, hid marijuana in my dresser drawer, got stoned in the john, stayed out after curfew, and slept with boys who had girlfriends so I could suffer the torment of rejection without the risk of intimacy. I began smoking three packs a day, lighting the next cigarette while the last one still burned, but nothing helped. I couldn't hide. The fantasy about catching the intruder found me.

I imagined different ways to capture him. I knock him out with a baseball bat. I have a gun. I find new methods to restrain him. He's strapped to a living room chair with duct tape. He's bound with a chain. After he's tied up, I wait to accost him with how much he'd terrified me. But as soon as he regains consciousness, his head sinks and he begins to weep. His tears are cloudy and abundant. He begs me to release him.

I never want to. I want to make him pay. But I can't stop myself. Fantasy after fantasy, no matter how determined I am at the beginning to hold on to the attacker, I unfasten his bonds and let him go.

# REBELLION

# 8

I dropped out of college at the end of my sophomore year, not surprising, since I'd never really checked back in. It felt absurd to attend an all-girls' school with Victorian sensibilities so divorced from the throb of the real world that we had to wear skirts to dinner.

Manhattan had been the most exciting place on earth when I was in high school. I moved there, finding everything I needed through classified ads in *The New York Times*: a nonprofit book company seeking a receptionist, a girl from Chicago looking for a roommate, a walk-up flat in an old brownstone on the Upper West Side.

I linked up with the boy I'd showed my scar to that night back at the Student Center, first out of attraction and then for convenience. Paul no longer sold drugs and now, armed with his liberal arts degree, went to work at one of the few places that welcomed any college graduate. He became a social worker in Manhattan. He asked if he could bunk in my apartment until he got settled, and I'd agreed. But after he moved in, he never left, sharing the rent and contributing handyman things like constructing a plywood wall to give us extra privacy and painting my bedroom ceiling black to look like the night sky.

I never planned on staying with Paul—he had the same caustic nature as my brother—it was just easier. After a year, when we'd soured on the cockroaches and grime, we were drawn to the un-New York, San Francisco, a place supposedly so balmy and free, young people slept in the parks. It was 1968, the summer after the Summer of Love, and we drove across the country in Paul's VW bus, agreeing that we'd go our own way once we made it to the Pacific. But we didn't. Housing turned out to be more expensive than we'd expected. It made sense to find a rental together.

There was another reason I stayed. I was afraid to sleep alone. Ever since the attack, I couldn't make it to morning unless someone was nearby. If a branch scraped against the siding or a squirrel scurried across the asphalt roof, I'd wake suddenly, my heart racing, my throat tight. The man who attacked me had never been caught. He could still be out there trying to hunt me down or there could be another stalker just like him. I knew the likelihood of being preyed on in bed again was small, but that didn't cut the fear.

I enrolled in a local college, ready to continue with my education just as the school shut down. That fall, rows of riot police, visors covering their faces, shields in one hand and clubs in the other, surrounded hundreds of students gathered in the center of campus. The students were chanting and carrying signs, demanding a black studies department, something that made sense to me in theory but felt like a great inconvenience to my plans. At the time, although I believed in ending the Vietnam War and achieving racial fairness, politics didn't mean much to me.

That changed the following year, when I took the first class offered at the university on women's issues. Suddenly, all kinds of things made sense. I understood why the jobs listed under "Help Wanted: Female" in *The New York Times* had been the only ones I could apply for, why the catcalls from construction workers on the way to an off-Broadway play felt like spitballs, not compliments, and why the police never bothered to run a trace on the fingerprints the attacker left on the wall in our den.

Another girl from the class and I organized the first symposium ever held on campus on gender issues, billed then as a teach-in on sexism. More and more women started talking, meeting in each other's living rooms or in the industrial section of San Francisco at a makeshift women's center squeezed between a flophouse and a muffler shop.

The women's movement also locked me in with Paul. I'd gone from being a girl with folk-singer length hair and birth control pills in her macramé purse to someone who slapped printed stickers that read "This is another example of the way society exploits women" on movie posters with caged go-go dancers in mini-skirts and white boots. For me and most of my friends in my weekly discussion group, the guy we were with before we stopped shaving our legs was the one we were stuck with now. I resented the skirmishes about shared housework or how much sex I owed Paul every week, but I knew it was unlikely I'd find anyone else. So, for several years, I went to college, majoring in photography in the art department, residing with Paul and living for the women's revolution.

# 9

I f I could have been anything in the world, I would have been a filmmaker. I'd loved the mix of light and shadow, shapes and sounds in movies since I was a child. Now I longed for the chance to tell the stories of real women's lives. The art department offered only one film class and it had a long waiting list. My name had been working its way up the roster for over a year. In my last semester before graduating I finally got in. This would be my only chance in my college career, probably in my entire life, to have access to a 16mm Bolex movie camera with top-of-the-line Schneider lenses.

Walking into class the first day, I felt instantly comfortable. This was the room where I'd taken so many photography courses, with the darkroom in the back and the biting, sour smell of fixer hovering in the air.

Even ten minutes early, the room was full, but I didn't see anyone I knew. Worse yet, I realized as I scanned the faces, I was the only woman. How was that possible? Most photography classes were half female. An overwhelming male presence saturated the air with a simmering locker-room heat.

The instructor, Bob Collins, hurried in fifteen minutes late. His shirt was rumpled and stuck out in the back where he must have missed tucking it into his pants. Dropping a stack of papers on the table, he tried to flatten his springy hair with both hands before looking up at the class. He seemed about twenty-five, just a few years older than I was. With his freckles and turned-up nose he looked friendly, the kind of boy who grew up playing fetch with a beagle.

For the first hour, Bob told us what to expect and how we'd work, and that by the end of the semester everyone would create an original film. Before going into the second hour, he said we'd take a short break, then, almost as an afterthought, he called out, "Wait a minute." Reaching into his satchel, he pulled out a small purple book and tossed it to a guy in a fringed leather vest sitting off on his right. The student caught it with one hand.

"There are lots of ways to create motion," Bob said. "Here's a little piece I put together that shows one of the earliest techniques. Flip books have been around a long time. Edison was one of the first to use it. Okay, see everyone back here in ten."

When I returned to the classroom before the end of the break, a lumberjack-size man with a thick red beard was leaning inside the doorway, flipping the pages on the teacher's book. A guy with a long ponytail stood next to him, watching the images go by. Both men were snickering.

"Hey, can I see that when you're done?" I said, eager to be part of the group.

The burly student turned and grinned. He glided his fingers through his beard as if he were easing out knots, all the while glancing up and down my body. His eyes paused at my chest. It took me a second to realize he was reading the buttons pinned to my vest. I wore them so often, I'd forgotten they were there. One showed the Statue of Liberty throwing a fist with the words "Sisterhood is Powerful" underneath; another read simply "Uppity Woman."

He shook his head, snorted and tossed the book to me.

"Here you go. Enjoy it."

The book was postcard size and its purple cardboard cover looked handmade. The photos inside were black and white. The first image was the back of a woman's head, her hair long and matted. In the next picture, the woman had turned so that a sliver of her white face showed, revealing a big pale sausage in her mouth.

*No, it wasn't a sausage. It was a cock!* I felt as though someone had hit me in the gut. I flipped the pages and watched her head bob up and down. The cock disappeared, then reappeared. The camera stayed in tight, showing her closed eyes, stretched mouth and strained features. In the last few frames, the lens pulled back, revealing that the woman was sucking on a dildo glued to something flat. The final image was a close-up of a grinning man, with the phallus jutting out of his forehead like a rhinoceros horn.

The muscles in my jaw locked down. *Jesus. What was the teacher thinking?*

We were still on break when Bob Collins strolled into the room and I jogged alongside him, clutching his book.

"Why did you hand this out?" I said, trying to sound neutral.

He turned toward me and angled his head to one side, the way dogs do when they are thinking.

"It's an example of a flipbook. It's a way to create the illusion of motion."

*Wrong question.*

"I mean, why this piece? It's insulting to women." My voice got louder and sharper.

He looked at my face, then down to my vest.

"It's humor," he said in an exaggerated tone.

"But there's nothing funny about it."

"It's a joke. It's... "

"It's pornography. It's a rationale to show a blow job," I said. I'd gotten angrier than I meant to but confident I was right.

"Lighten up. You women's libbers shouldn't take everything so seriously," Collins said, sighing and speaking over my head.

I turned to see two guys towering behind me. The red-haired man had his arms crossed over his chest and the guy with ponytail stood with his legs spread, his hands hooked in his back pockets, smirking.

I was almost shaking with anger, not sure what I should do next. I could grab my notebook and hunker down in the back corner. I could stomp out and never come back. But I wasn't going to do either. I'd waited too long for a chance to make a film. These jerks weren't going to drive me out. I trudged over to where I'd sat before the break, yanked out my chair and plunked myself in the first row, right in front of the instructor.

After class, all I wanted to do was get out of there. But as I headed down the hall to my locker, I noticed that a new art exhibit had been hung in the central corridor. There were twenty or so life-size lithographs of female torsos, each showing flattened breasts and splayed pubic hair in blood-red paint. I recognized the work of a student I knew from printmaking. He would sidle up to the youngest, most vulnerable-looking women in class and ask them to model for him. When they stripped in the back of the room, he slathered ink on their torsos and pressed a large printmaker's stone, much like an x-ray plate, against their body, forming an impression he could copy over and over. The rumor was that he came up with this technique because he was a horny guy hoping to get lucky.

I could feel myself growing larger and hotter as I slogged down the corridor.

The decapitated bodies looked like splattered tomatoes. This wasn't art. No, it was worse than that. This exhibit felt like a crime scene. *Why was the department showcasing this crap? What would happen if I ripped down every sheet?*

Someone had to stop it.

The art department offices were at the end of corridor.

Although the chairman's office door was usually closed, now, for some reason, it was open.

"Is Dr. Hallaway in?" I asked his assistant, stepping inside.

She looked up at me over the top of her bifocals as if the question exhausted her. Behind her, in a separate room, I could see the department chairman peering at papers on his wood desk.

"Never mind," I told his secretary, striding past her and into his office. "Excuse me, Dr. Hallaway, can I speak with you for a minute?"

He was in his fifties, slightly overweight, with sparse brown hair that was almost all gray, and wire-rimmed glasses. He had on chinos and a blue denim shirt, the same kind of proletariat outfit I'd seen him wearing around campus. I'd never spoken to Dr. Hallaway, but as he looked up from his desk, he appeared reasonable, kind.

I introduced myself as an art major, trying to inject a crisp, cheerful inflection into my voice.

"Yes. Nice to meet you," he said, offering a pleasant smile and gesturing for me to take the seat opposite him.

"I just saw the new exhibit in the hallway." I said, sliding my chair a little closer to his desk.

He nodded and leaned forward expectantly.

"It's offensive and sexist," I said.

I wanted to seem like an unbiased observer but my voice had already taken on an edge.

"What?" His gaze shifted to the papers strewn across the top of his desk.

"It's not art. There's nothing artistic about smearing paint on women's bodies." My jaw was tensing again.

"What?" He bit his lower lip and glanced back at me.

"Men use women's bodies for all kind of reasons. To sell

products, to gain control... "

"I don't understand what you're saying."

"That exhibit is degrading to women."

"I don't understand." His eyelids began to flutter behind his glasses.

"You are the head of the department. You can determine what goes up on the walls. That exhibit has nothing to do with art. It exploits women." I was talking fast now, my words surging out like a marching band.

There was a long pause. He stared at me.

"I like women," he said finally in a tiny voice.

"What?"

"I do. I really like women. I always have. I have two daughters. I have a wife."

He stood slowly and, with effort, pried a thick worn wallet out of his back pocket.

"Look. See. Here's a picture of me with my wife and daughters."

He held it out to me and nodded hopefully. I felt compelled to glance at it.

"Nice family," I said faintly.

Dr. Hallaway walked around his desk to where I was sitting and I immediately rose to face him, coming up to his chest. Placing his hand lightly on my shoulder, he said, "My mother is alive. I'm very close to her. She's a wonderful woman." He patted my shoulder. "I've always liked women. Really. You have nothing to worry about."

Before I could form a reply, he leaned down, grabbed his briefcase and raced out the door.

# IO

By the time I climbed into my old VW bug to start the long drive home, I wasn't sure what to feel. The encounter with the dean had such a dreamlike quality, it was hard to believe it had happened. Unlike the morning's film class, it was actually funny. The more I replayed the conversation in my mind, the more hilarious it seemed. I looked forward to relaying it to my friends in my women's group later that week. I could already hear Jane's sweet giggles and see Cathy rocking from side to side, laughing while her dangling earrings swayed.

By the fifth red light in a row, boredom set in. Traffic was worse than usual on this congested part of Nineteenth Avenue, one of the least interesting streets in San Francisco. At best, my commute across the length of the city, over the Golden Gate Bridge and halfway across Marin County, absorbed an hour each way. Today was clearly going to be much longer. With one hand on the wheel, I groped inside my purse until I found what I was looking for. My cigar.

This wasn't one of those thin cigarillos. They were a waste of time, too dainty and unassuming. The cigar I fired up was eight inches long and extruded smoke like a coal-burning plant.

When people asked why I smoked cigars, I'd reply curtly that I enjoyed them. I'd never confess that I barely tolerated their taste any more than I'd admit their real appeal, their satisfying heft in my hand and the way the tobacco crunched when I rolled the body between my fingers. I liked how they acted as an exclamation mark when I gestured with one, underscoring what I was saying and making it seem more important. But most of all, I smoked cigars because it was an open act of rebellion—a little woman waving around the smelly, smoldering symbol of male privilege.

The cigar kept me company on the long crawl through San Francisco. By the time I could see the blue-gray waters of the bay, the orange pillars of the Golden Gate Bridge and the green knolls of the headlands on the other side, I was down to the stump. I yanked open my ashtray but it was full of sunflower seeds husks, the detritus from my real addiction. *What should I do? Could I throw it out the window?* I'd seen men toss butts out of cars lots of times but I hating littering. I was the kind of person who ran after supermarkets fliers when they blew off someone else's windshield. Anyway, a cigar wasn't actually litter, it was plant matter. *Who was going to notice anyway?* I flicked the stogie out my window.

The siren started as soon as it hit the asphalt.

In my rearview mirror, a motorcycle cop suddenly appeared behind me. His helmet was brilliant white like an enamel marble. His sunglasses were aluminum mirrors and the chrome on his bike glinted. He lifted up a big black-gloved hand and jabbed a finger in the air, pointing to the side.

I pulled over to the grass shoulder. Then, as he swung in, I started to open my door, thinking it would be easier to explain what happened face to face.

"Stay in your car," I heard him bellow. I slammed the door shut and shrank down in the seat.

I watched in my mirror as he kicked down his stand, climbed off his motorcycle and jiggled his belt down lower on his hips. He seemed to be taking a long time getting himself ready. Cars raced past us on the thoroughfare, their wheels sending a vibration through my floor. Finally, the cop marched toward me, growing larger in my mirror with each step. His black leather jacket was zipped up to his throat and his tan pants were as tight as leotards on his heavy thighs. Only the lower part of his face showed, and I saw rough pink checks and thick cracked lips. He could have been twenty-five or he could have been forty. There was nothing exposed to reveal his age.

He bent down alongside my door, making a rolling gesture with his fingers that I assumed meant I should crank down my window, which I did. Looking up at him, I saw a funhouse version of myself in his sunglasses, a big head wobbling on tiny shoulders.

"Do you know the penalty for littering?" he said, leaning in close to my face.

"I didn't think I was littering," I said softly.

"What the hell is a cigar?" He was almost shrieking.

I considered mentioning that a cigar would decompose but stopped myself.

"Do you know what the fine is?" He straightened up and I found myself facing the clasp of his belt and the handle of his gun.

"No, I don't think I do."

Of course I did. There were signs posted all along the freeway, proclaiming a five-hundred-dollar citation. I looked down at my hands, trying to mask my expression. I was always a terrible liar.

"Take out your license and registration."

I removed the forms from my purse and the glove compartment and held them out to him. He grabbed the papers at the corners, as though even with his hands encased in leather, contact with me was repugnant.

He stared at the license, then back at me. In the picture I still had hair down to my waist. Now it was hacked off at the ears, like the little Dutch boy on paint cans. I smiled up at him hopefully. *See, it's me. Harmless, contrite, twenty-two-year-old, child-like, five-foot, hundred-and-ten-pound me.*

He stomped around toward the back of my car and I turned in my seat to watch him. This was my latest VW bug. It had started as a faded blue junker with encrusted cylinders, a dented hood, crumbled fenders and no hubcaps. Paul had rebuilt the engine for me, then found two dinged but usable fenders in a junkyard. The car ran but it looked sad, with a white fender on one side and a yellow fender on the other. I bought a dozen cans of paint and sprayed the whole car flat black, thinking it would create a sleek, sophisticated appearance. But the paint pooled in the dents and accentuated them. When I was done, the car looked like a giant prune on wheels.

The cop stood in front of my rear bumper and stared. Paul had built a replacement out of two-by-four-foot lumber. The license plate was bolted to the wood, flanked by bumper stickers that read *Sister* and *Women Unite*.

For what seemed like a long time, the cop stood behind my car without changing his position, his legs spread wide apart and his hands on his hips. Finally, almost in slow motion, I watched as he raised one leg, bending it at the knee. For a moment, I thought he was doing some kind of stretch. Then he drove his heel into the trunk lid and the car lurched forward. He lifted his leg again and slammed his heel into the bumper, hitting it so hard that I wondered if the wood would crack. I swung around in my seat, facing forward, because somehow it seemed safer not to look directly at him.

A minute later, I heard the sound of gravel crunching and saw the cop's torso appear in the passenger window.

"God damn it," he said, as he punched the roof with the side of his gloved fist.

"Crock of shit," he said, kicking the front tire.

*Was I in danger?*

The little car jerked back and forth. *No, I'd be okay.* It was the beginning of rush hour. We were on a main thoroughfare and this was San Francisco, the kind of place where someone would notice if an officer of the law dragged me out of the car by my hair.

*Was this even legal?* It couldn't be, but that didn't matter. No one would believe me if I filed a complaint. My car was dinged up already. It would be my word, a crazy feminist, against his.

Actually, what he was doing might turn out all right in the end. If he kept pummeling the car, maybe he'd work out all his fury instead of fining me.

I pressed my hands down on either side of the seat to steady myself and waited.

Finally the motion stopped. Then the cop appeared at my door. His face was hysterical red and his helmet seemed too small for his head. He punched one hand into the flat palm of the other, over and over, before he spoke.

"Don't you ever, ever let me see you again," he said, finally. His voice was high, as though the strap under his chin was choking him.

He leaned toward me through the open window and the leather on his jacket crackled.

"Not for anything ever again," he said. "Do you understand?"

"Yes, sir, I promise," I replied, as he righted himself.

He kept his hand in a fist but he released one finger, his index finger, and shook it at me. I wasn't exactly sure what that meant but I assumed he wanted me to wait until he pulled away.

He stomped back to his motorcycle and revved the engine. He swung out, arcing the motorcycle so close to my car that pebbles sprayed my windshield.

I edged out behind him. Minutes later, when he peeled off at the last exit before the toll booth, I realized how tightly I was clutching the steering wheel and loosened my grip.

# II

Maybe most people would have been scared if they'd been trapped inside their car while a cop pummeled it, but I wasn't. And not because I was brave. It was just that my fear had no need to seek me out in new locales. It knew where to find me—in my own bed, in my own home, in the dark—any night it wanted.

That night, I dreamed a variation on the same nightmare that had clung to me for years. This time I was being chased through dark streets, past locked garage doors in a run-down commercial neighborhood. I heard a hollow clanking sound, as though the man pursuing me had knocked over empty trash cans as he ran. I tried to surge ahead but, no matter how hard I pushed, the thud of his steps grew louder, closer. In the distance, sirens wailed in the high-pitched sound of bees but there was no one on the street to help. My heart seized in my chest. I didn't think I could get away.

I forced myself awake. For a few seconds I didn't know where I was, then I heard a soft off-key jingle, like dented bells, and recognized the sound of the tags on my dog's collar. I looked down and saw Shirley, my white German shepherd, sitting on her haunches on the floor staring up at me. From the intensity of her gaze, I must have been moaning again in my sleep. I reached down and scratched the coarse fur on the back of her neck. Outside something snapped. I stopped petting my dog and held very still, listening. Shirley seemed to sense what I was doing. Her ears, large for her frame, angled forward and her body stiffened. The refrigerator groaned on the floor above us. A car squealed around a corner somewhere down the hill. Paul's breath made a wheezing sound. There was nothing unusual, no cause for alarm.

I took a deep breath, feeling the tension ease out of my jaw. I turned to look at Paul, lying away from me, facing the wall, still asleep. The blades of his shoulders extended out from his thin back like arrowheads.

"It's okay," I whispered to my dog.

When I leaned over to stroke Shirley before drifting off, the last thing I saw was her black eyes open, watching.

Shirley was always on guard. She despised anyone in uniform and distrusted most men. She threatened telephone repairmen, bank guards and off-duty bus drivers.

The men in our couples group probably assumed I'd selected a man-hating guard dog when they came to meetings at our house. No doubt the toll collector on the Golden Gate Bridge thought the same thing when he saw my bumper stickers and a German shepherd pressing her snout against the almost closed window, snarling as I threaded the dollar bill though the crack in the glass.

But they would have been wrong. Paul once saw a white German shepherd running by the ocean at Stinson Beach and was struck by its beauty. He selected the breed. He found the ad in the newspaper. We both choose the alert little female from a litter of six pups. I didn't know Shirley would grow up to be so protective and fierce. I'd just been lucky.

A few months later, Shirley crouched by my side in our open doorway, a deep growl rolling in her chest and her lips raised just enough to expose her fangs. Outside, six feet away, a man with wire rim glasses and bushy brown hair stood motionless, his eyes fixed on my dog.

"Don't worry, she won't hurt you. She's never bitten anyone.

She just acts vicious," I said in a breezy tone.

He picked up the backpack at his feet and took a step toward me. Shirley lunged a foot closer, her bark ripping out of her like water from a burst pipe.

"Shirley, be quiet. That's enough," I said, but I couldn't help thinking, *Good dog.*

My father had called a month earlier to ask if it would be all right if Marilyn's oldest son, a medical student, stayed with us when he came out to the West Coast over spring break. It had been easy to say yes because I liked my father's new wife. Now I patted Frank's arm in an exaggerated movement.

"See? He's a friend. Calm down now, Shirley. Stop it."

My dog stared at me with amazement. This was a strange man, after all. She stopped barking and looked from me to Frank but she didn't budge. Maybe she was waiting to see if I would change my mind. When I didn't, she dropped her head, turned and walked slowly to the kitchen, her nails clicking against the uneven plank floor.

"Sorry about that, Frank. Now that she knows you, she'll be fine."

Paul had been sitting in the living room, not far from the front door, reading a manual on rebuilding Volkswagen car engines. He eased himself off the tan futon that doubled as our couch, greeting Frank with the same expression he wore for most people, wary and critical, but faintly amused. Paul was wired at a high frequency. No matter how much he ate, he stayed fishing-pole thin. Frank and Paul were the same height, about five feet eight, but my stepbrother appeared spongy while everything on Paul came to a point.

"Hey man," Paul said, "How you doing?"

"Good," Frank said. "Listen, I appreciate your letting me stay here."

"No problem," Paul said. I nodded, as though we regularly had people coming through our tiny rented house on a dead-end street an hour north of San Francisco, when, in fact, in the four years Paul and I had been together, Frank was our first overnight guest.

Our house must have been built as a summer cottage. It was the only way the two-story design could be explained, but even then, it didn't make sense. The main floor had a central room, where we had an oak dining room table and a futon couch, a kitchen the size of a closet with a cracked tile floor, and a narrow bathroom with a tub, but no real shower. Until Paul cut a hole through the living room floor and built a ladder out of lumber, we had to go outside and around the house every time we wanted to use the bathroom.

Downstairs were two small rooms, one behind the other. Both had French doors, an inexplicable bit of elegance, that opened onto a deck, gray with mold. Paul and I slept in one room; the other had been converted into my darkroom.

A few nights later, Frank drove to San Francisco to visit friends, saying he wouldn't be back until late, if at all. Around eleven o'clock, Paul climbed down through the trap door to go to bed but I wasn't ready for sleep. I'd shot some photos of sunlight on the ocean that I was eager to see, and this seemed like the perfect, quiet time to develop film. My chemicals and running water were in the bathroom.

I went in, got my materials organized, scratched Shirley's ear as she settled on the tile floor and closed the door to the tiny room. Then I perched on the chipped white toilet lid, balancing a specially designed lightproof bag on my lap. The pouch had sleeves that came up to my elbows, sealing off my hands and forearms in the chamber. Everything I needed to get the film ready was inside the bag: a light-tight aluminum canister, four metal reels that fit inside it and a can opener. The bathroom light was on but it didn't serve any purpose. Everything was done by feel. I'd be working blind.

I pried the top off a film can and uncoiled the first celluloid strip, easing the edge of the film into the narrow grooves of a reel. It was a slow process, easy to get wrong, which meant I'd have to start over. But this time the first roll looped around without any problem.

Shirley gnawed at an itch on her leg. She shook her head and jingled her tags. She licked between the pads on her paw.

I had started on the second roll when I heard the front door ease open and footsteps in the house. I stopped winding the film and listened. Someone was moving around out there. Frank must have come home early. Any moment he'd turn on a light and yell *Hi*. I waited, staring at the thin line of black beneath the bathroom door, expecting it to brighten. It didn't. The floorboards groaned. It had to be Frank. He'd forgotten where the light switch was and was groping around to find it. *It's over by the front door, Frank. Just walk over there and turn it on.*

Outside, the living room stayed dark. The footsteps crept into the center of the room and stopped. My hands were sweating inside the pouch. Minutes went by. That's when I knew it wasn't Frank. He wouldn't sneak around in the dark.

I held very still, as if the slightest motion would give me away. *What should I do?* If I pulled my arms out of the sleeves, light would pour in and scar the emulsion of the film. I didn't want to lose my shots. There was an intruder in the house and I was pinned.

I listened as the footsteps receded. *Where was he going? Was he over by the window? No, he was moving around the room on the balls of his feet.* A tinny sound. *Did he have keys chained to his belt?* Creeping, then soft clanking, then quiet. *What was he doing?*

He was searching for something and not finding it.

I looked down at Shirley, then over toward the door. She followed my gaze and sat up. *Why wasn't she barking?* The floorboards squealed louder. The bathroom had become a pressure chamber and the air was crushing me. I stared hard at Shirley. Her black eyes gazed back into mine. She cocked her head toward me. *Couldn't she sense what was happening? Didn't she smell him? Bark, Shirley, bark! What was wrong with her? She was a German shepherd. This was what she lived for.* But she just sat there, watching me.

Paul and Shirley were supposed to be my barricade, my protection plan. Now it was all unraveling, like the film lying loose in the bag and sticking to my hand. The steps moved closer. The intruder knew I was here. He'd found me again after all these years. The doorknob started to turn.

I screamed. It poured out of me like lava erupting down a craggy slope, the same agonized voice I'd heard the summer I was eighteen. My hands rushed out of their trap and covered my ears, as though my own voice was deafening me. Shirley ran in small circles, gulping while she barked, agitated, almost biting the air.

"What is it? Are you all right?" The voice was high and frightened on the other side of the thin door.

I pulled in one long breath, then another.

"Frank?" I whispered in a scratchy voice.

"Yes."

"I didn't know it was you. Why didn't you turn on the light? Why didn't you say something?" I could feel parts of myself reassembling.

"I thought everyone was asleep. I didn't want to disturb you. I was just coming over to use the bathroom."

I opened the door and slunk past Frank into the living room, noticing how spongy the floor felt under my feet. I switched on the brass floor lamp, the one I'd recently rewired, steadying myself against an armchair with one hand. Shirley stayed close beside me, trying to comfort me, nuzzling my other hand open, licking my palm.

"You scared me, that's all. I thought someone broke into the house." I tried to make my voice sound ordinary but it wavered.

Frank stopped ten feet from me, parting his lips, starting to say something but stopping. I glanced over at his chalky face. *That is how I must look, waxy and white.*

The next morning, Frank had his duffle bag packed by the time Paul and I came upstairs for breakfast, saying he was ready to hit the road sooner than planned and thanking us for our hospitality. I figured he wanted to get as far away from me, from the crazy lady, as he could and I was glad he was leaving. I felt ashamed he had seen me so weak.

# 12

As soon as Paul and I walked into the classroom for the film finals in June, I knew something was wrong. The air in the room felt slippery. I glanced around to see what was different. The men were talking to each other in clusters of twos and threes like they usually did, decked out in the familiar red bandannas, beaded denim jackets and cowboy boots. The walls were still painted the sour green of hospital emergency rooms. The metal cage was still closed and locked over the checkout window. The fluorescent light that had blinked all semester was still sputtering. Everything was the same. I tried to shrug off my edginess, figuring I must be sensing people's anxiety about the upcoming critiques of their work.

The film class had remained a battleground for me all semester. I didn't show up every Tuesday and Thursday seeking confrontation. In fact, I hated it. But it was my duty to speak out. So every image of a nude female, every depiction of subservience, became a teaching opportunity. I knew I was violating a common-sense principle of the women's movement: never take on a group of men alone. But what was I supposed to do—fold my hands in my lap and stay silent?

I'd assumed that other students would bring the people who'd worked on their films to the screening, but it turned out I was only one who had. Paul had logged in many hours as my cameraman and audio technician, and we'd made a really good film—feminist, yes, but irreverent, dark and quirky. He'd wanted to come to the showing, expecting some of the credit. That was fine with me because I was pleased that my boyfriend, with his keen sense of what was wrong with almost everything, was proud of what we'd achieved.

As we sat down, I thought there might be a problem that Paul was there. But Bob Collins, the instructor, started the class without commenting on his presence—maybe because, with his Afro hairstyle and worn jeans, Paul looked like he belonged.

Bob reviewed the rules for the finals. All fifteen students, going in alphabetical order, would have a chance to show their work, but because time was tight, we'd move quickly from one film to the next without any discussion. He added that no one needed to worry how their projects would be graded. Since everyone had completed a film, each of us was assured an A.

The first film didn't have a clear plot. It consisted of long shots of a railroad yard, a man darting between the cars and two men chasing him with guns.

When the film ended ten minutes later, Paul turned to me. "This is really boring. I'm going to see if I can find a Coke somewhere."

"Don't you want to be here for our film?"

"They're still calling names beginning with B. At this rate, you won't go on for another half hour at least. I'll be back long before then."

I studied Paul's face before he walked out. His mouth was pinched in his familiar expression of disdain but I thought I saw something unsettling behind his eyes.

The students whose last names started with C showed their films; next the Ds went. A student rose from the back and ran his movie, a clay animation about two dogs raiding a refrigerator. It was a funny film, but I was the only one who laughed. When it was over I looked at the clock, twenty-five minutes had gone by since Paul left. Even if the soda machines in the art building were empty, it still couldn't take this long to find one nearby that wasn't. He'd been so eager to be here for the screening. Where was he? When my name was called forty minutes later, Paul still hadn't returned.

My opening consisted of a series of grainy mug shots: a defiant Al Capone, a sneering Baby Face Nelson, followed by a close-up of my lead, a tall woman in her early thirties with strong, weathered features. My male narrator said, "Of all the heinous criminals who stalked American streets, none caused more damage nor evoked more terror than Miss Mettler."

I'd only seen my film projected on a plaster wall in our house, never on a real screen. Seeing it so bright and large was amazing. It looked like a real movie.

In the first action shot, the protagonist sits at her desk in a bull pen filled with other secretaries. Her boss, a man with greasy blond hair—and a real manager at the health insurance company that had given me permission to shoot part of my student film there—drops a stack of folders on her desk, saying she'd have to work late. Her face registers resignation and exhaustion. Later, at home, she serves dinner to a boyfriend who never stops talking about himself. In bed, we see the boyfriend's back, doing the equivalent of push-ups on her body. When he collapses on her after coming, she stares at the ceiling, motionless.

One guy toward the front of the classroom shoved his seat back and the chair's metal tips made a gouging sound on the floor.

We were near the end of my film. Two people stand beneath a tree at night, their shapes hard to discern. There is a rustling sound; then the man, the boyfriend, screams in terror. A second later, the heroine shouts, "No more!"

Her form is visible now. She is clad all in black, cloaked in a long cape, leaning over the man's fallen body. As the camera pulls in for a close-up, she stares into the lens and smiles. Her hair is loose and wild. Her canines have grown into fangs and her lips are stained with blood.

I tried to gauge the class's reaction. I could make out Red Beard slouched down in his chair, legs stretched out in front of him, and the instructor perched on a stool near the light switch, but I couldn't see any faces. There hadn't been any murmuring during my showing, which was a bad sign, but my film wasn't over yet. My closing scene was the best part.

The last shot opens wide, back at the corporate offices where the film began. A long row of secretaries—all women employed by the real insurance company—are sitting at their desks, heads down, focusing on their work, as the narrator intones, "Authorities are trying to determine if this was an isolated incident or if more and more women will be resorting to violence."

The camera slides close to the first desk and the woman glances up from a stack of papers. Her gray hair is softly lit by afternoon light slanting in from the windows. She looks unsure. Then confidence settles into her features and, gazing into the lens, she smiles—not a tentative smile signaling acquiescence, but a sly, knowing grin.

I leaned forward in my seat, feeling a glow like sunlight on my face. I loved this scene! I couldn't believe I'd created something this polished.

In one smooth motion, the camera glides over to the next woman in line, a slender, middle-aged black woman with wide cheekbones. (Since we didn't have a dolly, I'd improvised one, wheeling Paul along in a chair with casters as he shot.) As the woman looks up, she draws her lips back into a smile, slowly, as if she were leisurely opening a curtain.

Down the row the camera pans, settling in on a plump woman in a striped dress, a thin girl with glasses, an Asian woman with an elephant pendant. One after another, each woman stares into the camera, her face filling the screen, and smiles.

When the lights came on, there was silence. For a moment, I thought the class might start to applaud. I got up, pulled my reel from the projector and went back to my seat in the middle of the room. I waited for the instructor to call the next student's name but nothing happened. The only sound was the thud of a drop of water from the faucet hitting the stainless steel sink.

Suddenly Red Beard shot up from his seat. "I knew it," he yelled. "I knew you'd show some kind of women's lib shit."

"Yeah," several men said somewhere behind me.

"I've been expecting this all along. Well, I've brought some slides to show what women are really like," Red Beard said, emphasizing the last few words.

*What was he talking about? This was our film class finals. Time was limited. The teacher wasn't going to let him take over the class.*

"That sounds good. Can someone set up the projector?" the instructor said.

"How can he show slides? This is a film class," I said, turning to Bob Collins.

"We can take a minute to see them. It's always good to evaluate another point of view," Bob replied, his tone as perky as ever, as he dimmed the lights.

The first slide showed a naked woman in her twenties squatting next to an open toilet. Her wiry brown hair buzzed out from her head and her skin, like everything in the image, had a yellow cast. She stared at the tile floor, her eyes glazed over. Rusty watermarks stained the inside of the bowl.

*This is so bizarre. The instructor will tell him to stop.*

"Nice shot. Really imaginative," Bob's voice called out.

The next image clicked into place. The same naked woman was now seated at a table with a dinner plate, an empty glass, a butter knife and a fork lined up in front of her. On the plate was an orange wax model of an erect penis. She stared at the object with the exaggerated, eager look of a Betty Boop cartoon.

"How'd you get that prop?" a man behind me asked.

"I was making moulds for a sculpture class. Then I had this inspiration and made it of myself one night."

"Very cool."

"Who is the model?" another man said.

"That's my girlfriend."

Click. The next slide came up. Drool slid down the woman's chin, as she held the knife in one hand and the fork in the other. She was about to slice into the wax penis and take a bite.

This felt like a dream. The muscles in my jaw seized up and I expected to hear something shatter. Red Beard was demonstrating how much he could degrade his girlfriend and I felt humiliated along with her.

"Hey, that's cool," one of the men said. "How'd you get the grain?"

"I used natural lighting and I pushed the film speed," Red Beard said.

"Can we stop this? This is misogynistic. This has nothing to do with our class," I said.

I'd slunk down in seat and my voice had a desperate quality. Didn't any of the men realize these were examples of the most hateful images of women ever created, as filthy receptacles for sex or devouring castrating beasts. Didn't they know how sick these pictures were?

"We've had to listen to your rants all semester," the guy with the long ponytail said.

"You think you know everything. You don't begin to know what art is. Why don't you shut up?"

"You can't take it, can you? You just dish it out."

Some of the men had slid their chairs closer, squeezing me in the center. I could smell someone behind me.

Click. In the last picture the woman pretended to be eating, her eyes closed in mock pleasure, her cheeks distended. A headless shiny cock lay on her white dinner plate. Her breasts drooped just above it, sad and flat against her skin.

By the time the lights came back on, my breathing had grown so shallow, I wasn't sure any air was reaching me. *Stay seated*, I told myself. *Don't run out of the room. Don't let them see how angry, how afraid you are.*

The instructor sauntered down the aisle. "Thank you for sharing your work with us, Ron. I appreciate your bringing it in. That was very interesting. Now, who is next?"

I wasn't aware what was on the screen when Paul finally strolled in—his slow gait, his cool walk—holding a red can in his hand. It had taken him two hours to find that Coke. How had he known to hide?

When I told Paul what happened on the drive back, he didn't turn to look at me, keeping his gaze on the road even though the traffic was light going through Golden Gate Park. I wrapped my arms around my sides. My ribs ached as though I'd been pummeled.

"I can't believe you were walking around campus all that time," I said, struggling to find the energy to talk, my voice sharp despite its low volume.

"I told you. I just felt restless."

"That's hard to believe."

"Yeah, well, it's true."

"I wish you'd been there," I said, finally, all the irritation leaving my tone.

"Sorry I missed it," he said casually. Then he glanced at me quickly and I saw the tension ringing his eyes. "I doubt there was anything I could have done anyway."

*No*, I wanted to say, *you are wrong. If you had been there, I wouldn't have been alone. That would have made a huge difference.* But I didn't say it. We were crossing the bridge and the chill from the bay seeped in through the closed car windows. Paul was right. There was nothing he could have done for me because he'd been too afraid himself.

# DESTRUCTION

# 13

The karate school took up the lower floor of an old two-story stucco building on a one-way street that led to the freeway. When I entered at four in the afternoon, it looked deserted. The large room in front of me was dominated by a floor covered in worn green canvas and a wall covered with mirrors like dance studios I'd known. A huge punching bag with duct tape patches dangled on chains from a ceiling hook. On the far wall, fastened to fake wood paneling, were odd-looking weapons—a large curved sword, two short wooden sticks attached by a foot of rope and a pair of daggers with long, sinister, rounded blades. Alongside the weapons hung several pairs of yellow and red padded punching gloves and a matching helmet. Everything about this room proclaimed fighting and it thrilled me.

"Are you interested in learning karate?" a man's voice said behind me.

I turned to see a short, chunky man with brown hair falling almost to his eyes scurry out of a small room near the front door. I hadn't noticed it when I walked in. It must be the office. The man was wearing a white karate uniform with a faded black belt cinched under his ample belly. He wiped his hands on the front of the pajama-like canvas pants and fastened his mouth into a smile.

I straightened up reflexively. "I want to be able to defend myself."

The man tugged at the edges of his belt, pulling the knot tighter. "You've come to the right place," he said, introducing himself as Stan Hoffman, one of the owners.

At his suggestion, I followed him around the school, through what he described as the main workout room, past a smaller room where a lanky young man in a black karate suit and a brown belt stood with one arm extended, his hand in a fist, trying to demonstrate some move to two small boys happily shoving each other behind him. He glanced toward the door and nodded a greeting at Stan as we passed.

"Here's our changing room. And there's a shower you can use after workouts," Stan said when we came to the third room in the back, a makeshift space that had been built by erecting plywood walls inside a larger unfinished area. The door was closed and I could hear the voices of what sounded like teenage boys giggling inside.

So far, I hadn't seen a single woman. I wasn't going to sign up if I was the only one.

"How many female students do you have?" I asked Stan as we started to retrace our path on the worn brown carpet that ran alongside the training rooms.

"Quite a few," he said, stopping and partially facing me.

"How many would you say?"

"Maybe ten," he said, his voice dropping.

He seemed defensive about the number but I was pleased. It was more than I'd expected.

"Can a woman my size really defend herself?" I asked.

His shoulders dropped a quarter inch and he smiled. "Absolutely. *Kenpo*'s a great style for a short person like us. Let's go back to my office and I'll explain all about it," he said, turning and padding off.

We sat opposite each other across a large cluttered desk, the kind used by the principal in my elementary school. Stan opened a drawer and pulled out a brochure with an orange cover and a folded sheet stapled inside, showing me a list with names like "Eye of the Tiger," explaining that each represented a self-defense technique. I'd learn how to defend against all kinds of attacks: a wrist-lock, a choke hold, a full nelson. I could feel my enthusiasm growing by the second. My brother had ensnared me in wrestling holds when we were young and no matter how hard I twisted or squirmed, I could never get him off me.

Stan flipped open a large book, picked up a pen and, leaning forward, said, "When is a good time for you to start? The first three private lessons are free, so you have nothing to lose."

He had almost won me over. He'd said, "a short person like us." Like us, not like you. I wanted to say yes but I couldn't yet. I had to bring up the hand-painted signs in his windows. The one on the left side proclaimed "Self-Defense and Strength Training for Men and Boys," while the advertising on the right promised "Weight Control and Fitness for Women and Girls."

"I'm interested in studying here but I've got to tell you, the wording in your signs really puts me off. Don't you think women want to be strong and defend themselves?"

All the eager energy drained from his face and his voice faltered. "My partner and I talked a lot about what to say. There aren't many women in martial arts and we wanted to appeal to women." He looked down at his lap. "We thought we were saying something good. We thought women were always looking to lose weight. We thought they'd like that."

He wasn't hostile at all, insecure but not threatening or patronizing. I didn't have to keep my guard up.

I signed up for the first opening Stan had. The next day, when I drove past the school on my way to the freeway, Stan was balanced on a ladder outside, scraping the letters off the sign.

For the next two years I trained at the karate school about three times a week, but it wasn't until I was an intermediate student, a blue belt, that I learned my first knife defense.

"Will this really stop an attack?" I asked Stan after we'd gone through the new routine enough times to know I'd remember the moves.

"Sure. If someone lunges at you and thrusts a knife down like that. Trouble is, that's not how guys fight with knives."

He was still holding the rubber knife we'd used for practice, and now he started tossing it from hand to hand.

"See, they keep them lose like this." He danced around me. "They like to slash and cut."

He jabbed the blade toward me and I jumped back instinctively.

"How do you block that?"

"If a guy knows how to wield a knife, it's really hard. The best thing is just run away. If you can't do that, stay out of range. If you have to fight, get around behind them as soon as you can and take them down at the knees."

"Are we going to learn a technique for that?"

"Afraid not," he said, walking over to the wall and dropping the knife into a wicker basket that held fake weapons and old mismatched shin pads.

I followed.

"Stan, one more thing," I said to his back. "What do you do if you wake up and someone has a knife at your throat?" My voice had taken on a low, urgent quality. I'd waited a long time to ask him this question.

He turned, paused, then jabbed his big toe on the vinyl mat. "Nothing."

"What do you mean?"

"I mean you don't move! The knife is too close to the carotid artery. You're lying down. You're at a complete disadvantage. I don't care how good you are. You can be a tenth degree black belt. It doesn't matter. One slip and you're dead."

"So, what do you do?"

"You do what your opponent says and you bide your time. You wait 'till his guard is down. Then you try to get away."

He squatted down, picked up his clipboard, and ran his finger down the page, but before he could say anything about my next technique, I asked again in almost a whisper: "That's it?"

"Yup."

Stan began explaining *Wings of Silk*, but it was hard to pay attention. I wanted to spin in place until the room flew away. No one, not even a black belt, could have done better that night. I hadn't failed!

# 14

The Pit Stop looked like most bars, a row of stools facing a long wooden counter and behind it, a mirrored wall stacked high with bottles of alcohol, glistening in the low light. There were small round tables pinched into corners and in the back, a jukebox and a patch of unadorned wooden floor where I supposed a couple could dance, although in the months I'd been coming here, I hadn't seen anyone try.

Jane and I settled into the only two empty bar stools next to each other. But not long after we'd gotten our drinks, she said, "Let's split up for a while and see if we get lucky. I'm going to grab that table back there while it's free."

My best friend and roommate had pale blue eyes and translucent white skin. Her face was small and delicate, like the porcelain head of an antique doll, while her shoulders were wide and her breasts large for her frame, making her look fragile and rugged at the same time.

I nodded, noticing I still had a little buzz from the joint we'd shared before we left our apartment. Jane carried her drink to the table and within minutes a man joined her, decked out in the kind of denim work-shirt Jane had favored all the years I'd known her in the women's movement. Not long after, a lanky man with thick brown hair and a worn leather bomber jacket slid onto the stool next to me, ordering a shot of scotch. I glanced over at him, then back to my White Russian, a mix of cream and coffee as sweet as a milkshake. I took another sip. Tonight could turn out well after all.

I would never have thought of a bar as a place to meet men if not for Jane. I didn't like alcohol; no one in my family did. The only liquor in our house had been a bottle of sugary Manischewitz wine set aside for the rarely celebrated Jewish holiday. But when Jane and I started living together, she revealed a partying side I hadn't known existed, including a knowledge of cruising bars.

By 1972, after the puritanical dictates of the women's movement and five years with Paul, I coveted large doses of hedonism. I wanted easy, anonymous sex, without pretense or obligations—the kind men could have. But looking back, I know that wasn't all I was seeking. If it had been, I'd never have gone to the Pit Stop, my first time out, in a 1900s vintage, pale pink lace dress that trailed to my ankles. No, I was mining for a romance-novel encounter, a fireworks affair, a soul-mate. But after picking up one man who imitated rigor mortis during intercourse and another who gave me the clap, I was becoming skeptical that it was possible to meet anyone decent in a bar. I just didn't know where else to look.

I peered over at the man in the leather jacket next to me. He was clearly the most attractive man in the room. I was about to say something about the song playing on the jukebox and how lovely Roberta Flack's voice was when he cleared his throat and turned to me.

"I didn't take someone's seat, did I?"

I twisted partway around, arranging my features into a pleasant expression. "No, it's free."

"Good. Won't want to do that, would we? My name's Matt, by the way."

The irritation in his voice surprised me. Even saying his own name seemed to annoy him. How strange. *Had I misread him? Was he coming on to me?* I couldn't tell and now I didn't care.

"That's nice. Mine is Nina," I said to be polite, letting my smile drift away and turning back to my drink.

Matt shifted in his seat. "What do you do for fun?"

There it was again, that sarcastic edge, as if he already knew my answer and found it pathetic.

I couldn't help myself.

"I train in martial arts," I said, looking right at him. It was what I did for fun but that wasn't why I said it. I wanted to shock him.

"Yeah? Really?" He sounded bored. "How far are you from black belt?" He held up his empty glass for the bartender to see.

I shifted my gaze back to my drink and muttered, "Let's see. There's green, then three degrees of brown, then black."

"Really? Too bad. Long way to go," Matt said, reaching for a handful of shelled peanuts and stuffing them in his mouth.

*Stupid comment*, I thought, but I didn't reply. There was no reason to tell him that I was in no hurry because I wanted to perfect the moves, that I was the best woman fighter in my school, or that the guys in the dojo called me Mighty Mouse behind my back, a nickname I secretly savored.

Still, Matt and I continued to talk a little. He asked where I lived and, when I told him, said he could give me a ride home if I needed one since I was on his way. In most cases, if a man made an offer like that, I'd assume it was a sexual invitation and that if I said yes, we'd have a contract to jump into bed. But not this man—there was no heat radiating from him. I thanked him, saying I didn't need the lift.

It had been twenty minutes since Jane found her own spot and now the bar was crowded. I glanced in the mirror at the people milling behind me and through a space between bodies found my friend. She was still sitting with the same man in the work-shirt but it was clear from the way she kept fiddling with her hair that she'd written him off. When he got up and headed toward the bathroom, I watched a loopy grin come over her face as she spotted my reflection and signaled me to join her.

By now all the bar stools were filled. I asked Matt to hold my seat, then squeezed through the crowd and crouched down next to Jane, poking her gently in the ribs.

"Not your type, right?" I said.

She nodded.

"How about you? You going to get it on with that guy?" she said, peering at me through her new rimless, rose-tinted glasses.

I shook my head.

"You ready to head back?" She'd driven us over in her Volvo.

I envisioned our half-empty apartment less than a mile away. I didn't feel like going home yet, smoking more grass, foraging in the fridge and watching old movies on TV.

"I think I'll hang around here for a while. Worse case, the guy I'm talking to said he'd drop me off," I said.

It wasn't that late, only eleven-thirty. In the back of my mind, I imagined someone with fire still showing up. But a half hour later, nothing had changed. I was still sitting next to Matt, exchanging an occasional comment, when he stood up, rotated his shoulders in little circles and repeated his offer for the ride.

"You sure it's no hassle?" I said, rising from my stool.

"No problem at all," he replied in the same flat tone.

My living room was dark when Matt and I walked through the doorway. The wood floor glowed where the streetlight hit the bare boards. When Jane and I moved into the Victorian flat in San Rafael, twenty miles north of San Francisco, we'd planned on filling it with whimsical art, leafy plants and cushy chairs. In the four months we'd lived together, we'd furnished each of our bedrooms, yet only bought two pieces for the common space—a 1920s mohair couch and a matching chair. They'd seemed ideal when we found them at a neighbor's yard sale, but what had looked imposing next to a pile of baby clothes on a lawn shrank in our huge living room.

No sounds came from Jane's room. She must be lying on her bed, reading. It was too early for her to be asleep.

"Well, thanks for the lift," I said, stepping into the center of the room. My footsteps echoed in the open space.

"Sure thing."

I expected him to turn and leave but he just stood there, slouching against the door jamb. He was even taller than I realized in the bar, maybe six feet two inches. I barely came up to his armpits.

He stood up straighter, letting his fingers run up and down the zipper on his open bomber jacket. He seemed to be considering something. Whatever it was made him smile; at least the corners of his mouth turned up. He took several long strides toward me, stopping a few feet away.

"Listen. I need some money. I'm running short," he said in a low, slow voice.

Yellow flicks glowed in the pupils of his eyes. I felt a knot form in my gut.

"Money? I don't have any money."

"Come on," he said, stretching out the words. "I'm sure you can spare a twenty."

"No. I really can't." My voice came out in a whine.

He looked down, shifting his weight between his feet. For what seemed like minutes, he didn't move. Finally he said, "I'll bet they don't show you how to deal with this in karate."

And in one quick motion, he lunged straight at me.

In an instant, I ducked underneath his outstretched arm and darted in, close. My right hand shot up, seizing his throat just over his bony Adam's apple and clamping down on his windpipe.

He was much bigger than me. *This was crazy.* No, it wasn't. Jane was in the apartment. If I yelled, she'd hear me and charge in to help.

"You're wrong. They showed me how to defend against that. And they taught me how to do this." I squeezed the rubbery tube in his throat tighter.

Actually, this wasn't true. I knew it even as I said it. What I was doing wasn't a good karate move at all. I'd just improvised it. If my teacher saw me now he'd say I was too committed, too exposed, too vulnerable. And he'd tell me what he'd said almost every time I sparred—I was too small to go straight-on with a larger opponent. I should have stepped off to the side to counter.

But my choke hold was working! I hadn't known for certain that it would since we didn't make physical contact when we practiced self-defense techniques. Matt's windpipe was in my hand, his skin had turned the color of wet concrete and his eyes radiated fear. It was exhilarating. I didn't want to stop but I forced myself to let go.

He backed away from me, staggering slightly.

"Hey, listen, I didn't mean anything. I was just fooling around." He swiveled his head back and forth, loosening his neck.

Then he wiped his mouth with the back of his hand and said in a strained, pleading voice, "I could really use some money, even a little. I'll pay you back, I promise."

"I don't have anything."

I couldn't believe he was still standing there. *What did it take to get him to leave?*

"Look, I'll give you my ring."

He pulled at his finger and twisted off a ring with a turquoise stone.

"This is really valuable. You can hold on to it until I repay you," he said, holding it out and walking toward me.

The ring appeared heavy from a distance but when he pushed it into my hand, I realized it weighed almost nothing. It was just a fake, probably not even silver.

I started to tell him I had no use for his ring but stopped myself. His expression was so pained and desperate, it triggered an alarm. I had to help him.

I grabbed my purse off the couch and pulled out my wallet.

"Here's all I have," I said truthfully, handing him a five-dollar bill.

"Can't you spare more? Please."

I held up my wallet, showing him the empty sleeve. He snatched the money from my hand, hesitated, turned and was gone, leaving me with the phony turquoise ring.

*What should I do with this thing?* I wanted to dump it in the trash-can but I couldn't; what if he returned to pay me back and asked for it? It might have sentimental value to him. I dropped the ring in my pocket, thinking I'd have to keep it just in case.

I started walking through the apartment, switching on the overhead lights. The flat was laid out in a horseshoe shape and the last room on the end was Jane's. I tapped on her door, mentally forming the story of how I blocked his attack and choked him. I knew my friend; she was going to love this tale. But I didn't like the part where I handed him money. Instead of coming across as powerful, I capitulated in the end, giving him what he wanted all along. Maybe I wouldn't mention that.

I knocked again.

"Jane?"

There was no answer. I twisted the knob and peered in. The

room was dark. Her bed was empty. She hadn't come home at all.

A few nights later I dreamed I was standing in the narrow hallway in my house in Queens. My mother, father and brother were clustered together in a corner of the kitchen, clasping each other. They weren't fully formed, more like the early stages of a portrait painting before any color is applied.

It was nighttime and the hall was lit by a yellow light, wavering and intermittent. I felt pressure building, like the elongated moment preceding an explosion. Something was wrong. Suddenly I knew what it was. The attacker was waiting outside the door.

Then, in one move, he kicked the door open and revealed himself. It was Erich von Stroheim, the Austrian film actor and director from the 1930s, with a thick muscular body, a shaved head, a monocle, and a fencing scar running down his cheek.

I hesitated for less than a second before leaping at him and pummeling him. He came back at me with full force. We grappled with each other, rolling into a ball of blows that moved so fast we looked like a cartoon, a whirling circle with little stars shooting off of it. Finally, the movement stopped. I was on top of him, my right hand cocked in a fist by my ear, ready to nail him. But he was almost unconscious. I didn't need to hit him again.

For eight years I'd had nightmares about the attacker. This was the first time I wasn't running, the first time I'd ever seen him, the first time I'd fought back. It was the last time I dreamed about him.

# 15

We had planned on finding another roommate to share our apartment from the start. We had a third bedroom, a small converted porch off the rear of our flat, and since we couldn't afford the rent by ourselves, we were going to look for another woman—a single woman—no couples. Jane volunteered to advertise the space while I was in Mexico. (My mother had long ago broken up with Sidney and had invited me to visit her in San Miguel de Allende, where she was studying art over the summer.) When I returned a month later, a couple was ensconced in the tiny back room. The man, Mike, was the founder of a combination rock band and puppet theater called The Orange Zucchinis and the woman, Leslie, his fawning girlfriend. Both were wealthy dropouts from Ivy League schools. (When I asked why she'd rented to a couple, Jane swore they'd been the only ones who'd answered her ad.)

It was hard to decide what provoked me most about the group—their music, their marionette plays or their sense of entitlement. When I'd trudge home from my secretarial job at a lumber company, I'd find grubby guys, wearing round, blue, John Lennon shades and women in blouses made from Indian bedspreads bought at Cost Plus. The group would barely glance at me when I'd pass them in the living room—too busy staring at my TV, stoned and snickering, watching Eddie Albert complain to a pig about life in the country on a rerun of *Green Acres*.

I hated how the puppet people seized control of my home. But worst of all, the band took Jane. She'd become part of the entourage. I thought about moving out but I didn't have the funds to start over.

Finally, one Friday in early September, The Zucchinis were booked for a free afternoon concert in Golden Gate Park. For the first time, I'd have the apartment to myself for an hour, maybe more, after work. That day, as I typed up orders for pine and oak boards, I imagined having control of the bathroom, the comfort of soaking in a warm tub and the soothing silence of an empty house.

At quarter after five, I unlocked the front door and darted through the living room. I was so focused on using every minute that I was almost in the hall before I registered a rustling sound off to my right. I stopped, motionless, feeling muscles tighten in my back.

There, in the corner, I saw a man leaning back in the mohair chair, his face and the upper half of his body in shadow. Only his long legs were lit, stretched out in front of him in frayed jeans and cowboy boots. He seemed at ease, the way a cat does, relaxed and ready at the same time. I could feel him staring at me. He shifted forward into a beam of sunlight and smiled. I remembered seeing him in my apartment before, watching the band rehearse, with a pale, pretty blond woman at his side and a plump, droopy-eyed baby in a stroller near his feet. I even recalled his name because it was one of my favorites. Stephen.

Some of the tension eased away from my spine.

"You know, you could scare someone just sitting there like that," I said.

He shrugged, leaning back again into the chair and clasping his hands behind his head, all the while watching my face.

I glanced toward the formal dining room cluttered with tangled speaker cords, black drums, silver guitars and their spare plywood puppet house painted pumpkin orange. Jane or the couple must have returned home early and let Stephen in.

"Who else is here?" I asked, but it didn't matter. Whoever it was, my plan of getting home before The Zucchinis was ruined. I started to move toward my room, the one place in the apartment where I could be assured of privacy.

"No one," he said, leaning forward and giving me a half smile.

His answer made me stop and look around. He couldn't be serious.

"What are you doing here?" I asked.

"I was waiting for you. I was hoping you'd come home first."

It took me a moment to decode what he'd said because I'd already heard his reply in my mind. He was going to say he was here for Jane. She'd started using cocaine while I'd been in Mexico, sharing it and her bed with most of the band.

"Really? I didn't think anyone in your group even noticed me," I said, walking over to the couch and sitting five feet from Stephen.

"Sure. I've watched you lots of times walking up the drive when you came back from karate."

"How did you know I trained?" My tone brightened.

"I asked Jane. She told me."

How would he even know to inquire? He must have seen me carrying my uniform rolled up and slung over my shoulder.

He sank back into the chair's padding and smiled again, leisurely.

"Anyway, everyone's all over Jane but I told Bonnie, 'Forget the blond with the big breasts. Check out the little dark one with the muscular legs.'"

I couldn't remember anyone saying anything complimentary about my legs. My mother used to tell me I had peasant legs, strong with thick ankles.

I looked over at Stephen, starting to actually see him for the first time. He wore a black T-shirt and denim jacket over his lanky torso. He had wavy, long black hair that hung below his shoulders and thick, pouty lips like Mick Jagger. He looked back at me through half-closed eyes. He had to be at least six feet tall. My god, this man was sexy!

The afternoon light slanting into the room was thick and hazy. The charge between us was so strong, I could almost see it quivering in the air. A contented sleepiness started to creep into me, like the seconds just before a nap, but a realization zapped me awake. I'd been the last one to leave the apartment this morning and I always bolted the door.

"How'd you get in here?"

"Broke in. It wasn't locked." He pointed to the front window that faced the lawn. His tone was open, friendly.

*Broke in?* I felt limp, disoriented, as though a hypnotist had whispered the code word that put me in a trance. For what seemed like a long time, I didn't move or speak. Then I recalled something Jane had told me about him when she gave me a brief rundown on everyone in the band and their entourage.

"Did you really do time in prison?" I asked. My voice came out so low and silky I barely recognized it.

Something sparked and lit behind his gray eyes. He scanned my face before he spoke and when he did, he answered slowly. "Yes."

I leaned toward him, almost whispering "What for?"

"Burglary. I did time as a juvenile and later, eighteen months as an adult." He elongated his words in a low, soft voice.

I could almost smell him, a flinty scent like something that might combust. But I had to resist his pull. I had no problem with hopping into bed with someone I barely knew, but not this one. I imagined Stephen with one arm draped over the blond woman's shoulder and the other cradling his child. He was in a relationship and, no matter what, I didn't betray other women.

"Aren't you going with someone?" I said, sitting up and straightening out my tone.

"You mean Bonnie?" He stretched his arms over his head and arched his back. "We've been together off and on for a long time. That's true. But we both see other people. She's going with Bob from the band right now."

"What about the baby?"

"Keith? She says he's mine but I don't think so. Bonnie was sleeping with a number of guys when she got pregnant. It could have been any of them."

Well, if they weren't monogamous and it wasn't his baby and she didn't care, I wouldn't be doing anything wrong.

He shifted slightly in the chair, spreading his legs and easing his hands down into his lap. I followed the movement and saw that the denim in the crotch of his pants was worn thin. He watched me with half closed eyes and the hint of a smile on wide, full lips.

It felt as if all of the candles and incense in the apartment were burning, infusing the room with smoke and sandalwood. I'd never seen anyone as purely sexual as this man. We couldn't strip off our clothes in the living room because someone from the band could walk through the front door any time.

Then the perfect idea came to me. I rose slowly, stepped toward him and said, "I was just going to take a bath. Feel like joining me?"

I led the way, pushing open the bathroom door, instantly dismayed at how cramped and seedy the room was, with strands of dark hair clumped around the baseboard. Actually, it looked exactly the way it had since the puppet people moved in. But in my mind, only minutes before, I'd imagined us nuzzling in an oversized bath, plump folded towels on the sink and a gleaming room so large, the walls hadn't even appeared in my frame.

"Hang on a minute," I said, turning to him. "I want to clean this up."

I opened the cabinet underneath the sink, pulling out a can of Ajax and a desiccated sponge. Stephen squeezed in past me, stopping briefly to check himself in the medicine chest mirror, combing his hair back with his fingers. He took a half step over to the toilet at the end of the room, lowering the seat and perching on the edge. He reached into his jacket pocket and slid out a joint and pack of matches.

"How about we get a little mellow?" he said as he lit the tip.

He inhaled deeply and passed the joint to me. Our fingers touched in the handoff, our first contact. He grinned and I tried to smile back. I took a long gulp of smoke, held my breath, sprinkled the Ajax into the tub, moistened the sponge, exhaled and started scrubbing.

"How long have you known Mike and the band?" I asked, stretching to reach the grime on the far side. I suddenly felt obligated to make small talk.

"Bonnie and I met them in New York a few years ago."

"Is that where you're from?" I said.

"No, North Jersey. Can't you tell?"

"Yeah, now that you say it, I can."

His accent was so heavy, how had I'd missed it?

When I'd gotten the tub as clean as I could, I dropped in the stopper and turned on the tap. The hot water was lukewarm, no point in adding any cold. If the upstairs neighbor had showered recently, we'd be lucky to have a bath at all.

"This should be ready in five minutes, maybe less." I said, getting off my knees and sitting on the edge of the tub.

Stephen nodded, smiling at me lazily. I couldn't think of anything to say. Maybe it was the marijuana, but speaking suddenly seemed like a lot of work. I watched bubbles form as the spray hit the water, creating a little dancing circle. I'd never noticed how interesting bath water could be. I glanced over at him and saw him gazing out the window. It felt like an hour had gone by and the bathtub only had six inches of water in it. Finally, Stephen stood up and stretched, his fingers brushing the ceiling.

"Let's just climb in," he said, yawning.

"Okay."

For a moment, neither of us moved; then Stephen peeled off his denim jacket and I began unbuttoning my blouse. We stood a few feet apart, our backs to each other, hunching over as we undressed, suddenly so uncomfortable we could have been getting ready for a medical exam.

Stephen climbed into the water first, taking the good side of the tub, the one without the faucet. I eased into the other. We faced each other upright and rigid, angling ourselves to keep our legs from touching. I stared down at my hips and realized they looked huge in the water. I tried to lean back and relax but the spigot pushed into my spine and thrust me forward. I averted my gaze so I wouldn't have to keep looking at him, but when I finally peered over, he was staring down into the water, glum.

My head felt swollen and heavy. It had to be the grass. I was trying to think of something to say to end this when there were two brisk knocks on the door.

"Occupied," I yelled. There were clear privacy rules for the only bathroom in the apartment.

Mike, the leader of The Orange Zucchinis, strode in. He had stringy brown hair and oval granny glasses. His chin showed through the patches of hair on his beard, making him look like the class valedictorian trying to pass for a radical.

"Hey, I'm using this room," I said.

"I just need to get the nail clippers," Mike replied, but he didn't open the medicine chest. He plunked down on the toilet lid and glared at me, then Stephen.

Stephen sank down in the water, pressing his hands across his groin and twisting his mouth into an uncertain smile that made him look like a cartoon version of a person caught naked.

I had to make a quick decision. Which part of myself did I want to cover with my hands: breasts or bush? For some reason, breasts seemed much more personal so I folded my arms tight across my chest.

"You have no right to come in here," I said, trying to sound authoritative.

Mike pursed his lips together as if he were going to spit.

"What about Bonnie? Does she know about this?" he blared at Stephen.

Stephen's face turned red. He lowered his gaze to his crotch.

"Hey, we haven't done anything," I said. "We're just talking a little bath."

A muscle on the side of Mike's face jumped. He stared at Stephen as though he was willing him to rise, but Stephen didn't look up, he just hunkered further down in the tepid water. When Mike turned to scowl at me, I was ready for him, glaring back. He opened his mouth to speak, hesitated, and without saying another word, got up, slamming the door on his way out.

I looked over at Stephen. His hands seemed to have locked over his groin. I tried to smile but he didn't respond. I couldn't believe how much he had changed. I hadn't noticed that he didn't have any hair on his chest or how skinny he was. The knobby bones in his shoulders stuck out and his ribs showed. *This was a mistake. I didn't want him anymore.* But I wasn't going to back down now and let Mr. Zucchini think he could tell me what I could do in my own home. If we were in a tug-of-war for Stephen, I'd be damned if I'd let Mike win.

I stood up in the tub, feeling the water pour off me in rivulets as I reached for a towel, not caring anymore that I was naked.

"The bath is pretty much ruined," I said, climbing out. "We might as well go to my bedroom."

# 16

By the time I dropped my towel and climbed into bed beside him, Mick Jagger had returned. Stephen had a half smile, lowered eyelids and a stupendous erection. That night and for the months that followed, I slid into the dark with him.

I had never understood how sex could consume someone until Stephen. I'd imagine our heat while I was buying groceries or answering a phone call at O'Connor Lumber.

"Just a minute, I'll see if he's in," I'd reply before pushing the hold button on my console and turning to my boss, sitting five feet away from me in the one-room office.

"It's for you, Mr. O'Connor," I'd say to the middle-aged man with a crisscross pattern of broken capillaries along his nose and his cheeks. But what I really wanted to say to him was, "I got buttfucked yesterday. We had outrageous sex. There's nothing we don't do. How was your evening?"

Stephen and I made love therapeutically to start the day, fiercely when I'd come home from work and leisurely before going to sleep.

One Saturday morning that first month with Stephen, we had sex, smoked a joint and napped. I got up an hour later and showered. Stephen was still in bed when I came in, his long hair fanned out against my white pillowcase like black lace around his face. He watched while I hung up the almost-new terrycloth robe I'd found at a thrift store.

"Get back here," he said. His voice was hoarse.

Stephen lifted the sheet, showing me his arousal.

It seemed that all my life I'd been waiting for someone to want me like this. Sex with Paul had felt like a chore. He didn't desire me or, if he did, he hid it well, pointing out extra weight on my rear when I asked if he thought I was pretty. Now, here was this outrageously erotic man who got aroused just looking at me naked. And in response, I couldn't get enough of him.

Sometimes during sex Stephen referred to himself as *daddy*. I hadn't thought about where that came from until one night he turned to me in bed, stroked my cheek and asked if I could guess the one person in the world he'd most like to meet.

"I have no idea."

"Manson."

"Charles Manson?"

"You've got to admire him, the way he controlled women. Look what he got them to do, how much power he had over them. You know he had to be very, very good." Stephen's eyes flashed as he said this.

I pushed him away.

*He's puffing himself up. He wants to scare me into thinking that he's a bad, bad boy because he can evoke that psycho's name.*

"Yeah, sure," I said.

I looked at Stephen's skinny arms now propped up behind his head.

*He's all talk. I could take him.*

The year before, during the Manson family trials in 1971, I'd read an article that described how Charles Manson led each new woman who joined his group out to a hidden place, a cave somewhere, to initiate her. He'd make love to her, whispering over and over, "Daddy's here now." At the time, I couldn't image any power in that, at least not with most women, certainly not with me. The idea of having sex with my father, shuffling around the house in his sleeveless undershirt, boxer shorts and black socks, was repulsive. But when Stephen called himself *daddy* in the midst of sex, a cloak dropped over me and I could imagine what Susan Atkins or Squeaky Fromme felt. Here was the dark home that went back before I could judge my father's appearance, when all I knew was the sound and the smell and the warmth of him. Here was the word that reached straight down—past all the years—to the very seeds of desire.

One evening when we were lying in bed, Stephen suggested tying me up and whipping me in a voice as matter-of-fact as if he were asking when dinner would be ready. His words ignited a fire that was set to be lit ever since I'd read *The Story of O* five years earlier when I was nineteen. I nodded, barely able to meet his eyes.

"I need something to tie you up. What have you got?" he asked.

I jumped up and rummaged in a dresser drawer while he pulled his leather belt out of his pant loops. After handing him a scarf, I positioned myself on the edge of the bed, facing away from him and crossing my wrists behind my back. I felt heat radiate from my groin to my breasts. But after he bound my hands, pressure built up in my fingers and they began to throb. In an instant, the excitement dissolved.

"Hey, that's too tight," I said, not hiding my irritation.

Stephen quickly reached over and, after some fussing, managed to loosen then retie the knots.

"How's that?" he asked, a flicker of anxiety in his voice.

"Better."

"Okay. Get on the bed. Head down, on your knees." His voice faltered.

It was hard to climb up and change positions. I had to use my chin at one point to angle forward. Stephen must have had trouble standing on the mattress because I could feel it wobbling beneath me. Seconds after the motion stopped, I heard a snap and felt a burning sensation singe across my butt.

"Ow! That really hurts," I said.

"Sorry. What about now?" he said tentatively, flicking the belt much lighter.

"That's okay, I guess."

He proceeded to spank me at half speed, spinning a story about rounding up some convicts to use me. His fantasy was so unappealing I had to conjure up scenes from the medieval French castle in *The Story of O* to stay aroused. This was much more work than I'd imagined. After we had sex, I told him to release me and he hurried over to undo the scarf.

It wasn't just one night that we played out this scene. This charade became one of the staples of our sex life. Here—with a thief who'd broken into my house, who'd essentially been stalking me—I reenacted the times I'd been helpless. But with Stephen, I could pretend to surrender because I was finally in control. Unlike the afternoon my father choked my mother or the night the assailant pressed a knife to my throat, I could make this stop whenever I wanted.

# 17

Two months after they'd moved in, Jane and I told the founder of The Orange Zucchinis and his girlfriend to leave.

I'd hoped my old friend and I would regain our closeness after that, but we barely saw each other. Stephen was waiting for me every evening when I came home from the lumber company, and a new man Jane had met, a shy graduate student, showed up in the evening for her. Mostly we stayed in our bedrooms, running into each other at night in the kitchen. Sexual energy permeated our house, its yeasty smell rising over the incense and marijuana.

By early November, something shifted. One Sunday morning, I sat up in bed and poked Stephen in the ribs to wake him. I hadn't taken my dog, Circe, out for a long run in weeks and it was time. When I was at work, I boarded her during the day at an outdoor doggie daycare kennel so she could play with other dogs and get exercise, but weekends were my responsibility.

Circe was the granddaughter of the fierce German shepherd Paul and I had owned. Like Shirley, she had white fur, black eyes and a coal-dark nose, but in almost every other way, she was different. For one thing, she loved people. She'd watched The Zucchinis tromp in and out of our apartment with mild interest, never barking. In fact, she seemed to trust everyone except the occasional toddler who lunged toward her at eye level at the beach.

Getting Circe had felt like a little miracle. When Paul and I were together, Shirley had puppies. Later, as our relationship dissolved, she stayed outside for longer periods until one day she never came back. We searched, posted signs, offered rewards but never found her. It was heartbreaking. Then, a year after we'd parted, Paul told me he'd gotten a phone call from someone who'd bought one of Shirley's pups, saying their dog was now a mother and we were welcome to take our picks of the litter. Paul and I both chose little females. I was elated. I'd have a white German shepherd again, a descendant of the great Shirley, and this time I'd take better care of her.

I poked Stephen again and he opened his eyes slowly. It was about ten in the morning and the sunlight streaked in through my window.

"Come on. Let's go to Mount Tam. What do you say?" I said, sitting up.

Stephen didn't respond but he stretched one long arm over to the nightstand and snared a pack of matches and a joint in metallic gold tobacco paper. He lit up, sucked in the smoke and held the joint out to me.

"I don't like to get high in the morning. You know that."

He let out a long exhale. Then he reached down to the floor, grabbed my decorative pillow with the embroidered blue dragon, propped it behind his head and settled back against the massive oak headboard.

"It's Sunday, babe. Don't be so uptight. Celebrate."

It was always the weekend for Stephen since he didn't work. I stood up, walked to the window and opened it to let in some air.

An hour later, with Stephen alongside me and Circe in the back seat, I drove up the long, winding road to the one true mountain in the county, Mount Tamalpais. The peak was reputedly sacred to the Indians who'd lived there and now, as a

6000-acre state park, it remained largely undisturbed.

Circe paced back and forth in the rear seat, thrusting her head out my window, then Stephen's, until he rolled his closed, saying he'd had enough of a wet nose on the back of his neck. As soon as I pulled into a parking space and opened the door, Circe bounded out beside me.

Before I'd met Stephen, I often took Circe out to play. Sometimes I drove us to the Pacific, past the brown hills of the California dry season along a narrow road that snaked with turns. All the dogs I'd known loved the water but none like Circe. She didn't need me to throw a stick or a ball to motivate her. When we reached the sand, she'd race toward the ocean and charge in. And Circe not only swam, she leaped off piers fifteen feet into the sea and from huge boulders into swimming holes in forest streams. She was fearless.

Some days, I'd drive us to a park off the main street in Fairfax, a small town in western Marin where dogs didn't have to be tethered on a leash. I carried her Frisbee in one hand while she pranced by my side. When we got to the park, I'd tap the red plastic disk over my head to signal my readiness and she'd show me hers, jumping and yapping, her tail slapping wildly from side to side.

"Back up, girl," I said one day, holding the Frisbee over my head and stiff-arming her away with the other. She crouched in front of me, ears flat, but didn't move.

"Go on."

Circe backed up two feet without taking her eyes off the Frisbee.

"Further," I said, making a shooing motion with one hand.

She moved another five feet.

"Further."

Three feet.

"Further."

She went back a dozen more paces, spun in a circle and barked. We were now about twenty feet apart.

"Okay, ready, here it comes," I said, stepping into the toss and launching the Frisbee high in the air. Circe watched it soar, aligned herself with the trajectory and raced toward the flying disc. But once she was in place to catch it, she turned and began running in the same direction, as if she'd planned on beating it to the finish line. When she was about five feet in front of it, she leaped up, all four legs in the air, and as the Frisbee sailed alongside her, turned her head over her shoulder and—still aloft—caught it in her teeth.

From across the park, an old Chinese man in a traditional mandarin-collar shirt yelled, "How did you train your dog to do that?"

I was amazed as he was.

"I didn't. She taught herself," I shouted back.

I threw again. Within minutes, a small crowd formed. Two cars pulled to the curb and a few people climbed out. It seemed everyone wanted to gather around and marvel at my athlete.

Stephen and I followed a path around the crest of Mount Tam. I waved the Frisbee with one hand and looked down at my dog. Her black eyes were bright.

"Ready? Are you ready, girl?"

I lobbed the Frisbee down the slope and Circe sprinted after it. We continued on the trail, moving slowly since Stephen was a poor hiker, stoned and wearing sandals. Circe had no trouble finding us when she scampered up the hill, the disk in her mouth. We repeated this—me throwing the Frisbee, Circe charging after it, then Stephen and me ambling along. About fifteen minutes later, Stephen stopped and pointed.

"Look at that nice spot over there. How about we get it on?"

"Right here? Out in the open?"

He turned in a circle.

"Do you see anyone around?"

It sounded sexy, bad and romantic all at once—young lovers on a mountainside on a warm, clear day. I'd never gotten it on outside and this had an element of daring. Why not?

We tramped down the slope about forty feet off the path and picked a place. We didn't have a blanket, so I lay back in a clump of weeds. Stephen stood over me unbuckling his belt. Circe settled down a few feet away and dropped her head on her paws. She often napped on the bedroom floor while we had sex.

"Hang on. There are rocks sticking me in the back," I said.

Stephen dropped his pants to his ankles and reached over me, jiggling mine down as well.

"You won't notice them in a minute," he said.

He was wrong. One stone lodged itself in the small of my back and jabbed me as he entered. I opened my eyes and saw Stephen's squeezed shut with strain. My pants were scrunched down by my feet as though I'd been prepped for a gynecological exam.

"Can you hurry up? This is really uncomfortable," I said.

Suddenly, off to my right, I heard twigs breaking. Two men were strolling right near us on the trail but Stephen kept humping. Circe looked up, wagged her tail, then dropped her head back down. One man, with wild gray shoulder-length hair and a red bandanna around his neck, grinned at us.

"Right on," he yelled, looking down. "That's beautiful. Just beautiful."

The man must think it was still the Summer of Love and we

were flower children—all that crap I had wanted to believe but never trusted.

"This isn't a show, buddy. Get out of here," Stephen muttered, not loud enough for the men to hear.

"Keep it up, man. Peace," the gray-haired man yelled, as he and his friend moved on.

Moments later, I pushed Stephen off me, feeling too dirty and exposed to continue.

After that fiasco on Mount Tamalpais, I wanted to make love in the countryside and get it right. I also thought that if we could do something romantic, it might rekindle the sexual intensity that had started to slip away.

In December, after a storm had pounded the region with rain, a Saturday emerged dry, sunny and warm, one of those rare days that open like a bud in the midst of a northern California winter. This would be a perfect time to make love under some towering oaks. I wasn't about to go to a state park again, but some of the instructors in my karate school had been to our sister school in Santa Rosa and they'd raved about the town. Santa Rosa was about an hour north of us, the opposite direction from all the urban development—there were bound to be lots of woods there. After I told Stephen what I wanted to do, he nodded and climbed out of bed.

Circe had been lying on the floor of my room, watching me. When I finally pulled my navy wool jacket off a hanger, she sprang to her feet. She raced out of the room, sliding in the hall where she lost traction on the bare wood, but still managing to reach the living room before me. She pressed her nose into the seam where the front door met the molding as if she could already smell the outdoors. She lifted her front paws high, taking small dancing steps, gazing up at me, then at the doorknob, then back at me.

"Let's leave her this time. I don't feel like having her breathing down my neck all day," Stephen said.

It had never occurred to me that Circe wouldn't come. But it was winter; the days had grown shorter; there wasn't much time left that afternoon. I didn't want to waste it arguing.

I turned to my dog.

"We're just going for a drive. You stay, girl." I held up my palm.

Her prancing stopped.

"We'll go play soon. I promise."

I opened the door.

Circe sat on her haunches, staring at me. A thin haze drifted over her eyes.

We drove north on the freeway, passing turnoffs where we could buy burgers, gasoline or a Ford pickup. We rode by the Frank Lloyd Wright pink civic center that looked a 1950s science-fiction movie set. We passed cows standing in mud but no rustic spot that looked promising for sex.

My VW bug didn't have a radio. After half an hour, Stephen started tapping on the window glass with his fingertips. He retied his ponytail. He leaned his head against the back of the seat, stared at the roof of the car and starting picking at a tear in the fabric.

"Stop it! Don't make it worse," I said.

He pulled his hands into his lap, pursed out his lips and sighed.

"How much further?" he said finally.

I had no idea.

"Anytime now," I said.

He lit another joint.

"That's just going to make the time go slower."

He didn't answer. He sucked in the smoke and passed the

grass to me. I wasn't interested in getting high but it seemed a waste of good weed not to share it.

The further I drove, the more nature receded. Instead of the open grassland we'd seen earlier, aluminum warehouses flanked the freeway. Finally we reached Santa Rosa and a sign that read "College Avenue."

"There's bound to be some country outside the city limits," I said, tired of driving and relieved to turn off at the exit. "This is a small town."

Beyond an Arthur Murray Dance Studio and a twenty-four-hour convenience store, brick houses filled the streets in tidy rows. I turned right and right again. The houses were larger on this block and painted the colors of an infant's bedroom: pea pod green, robin's egg blue, baby chick yellow. I started to worry that we'd get lost. I didn't want to curve around any more roads because I'd need to find the freeway entrance to get us home. Stephen was useless at directions, at everything except sex.

I finally pulled over to the curb.

"Look, it's almost three o'clock. I'm ready to head back," I said.

Stephen had been pulling loose threads from a tear in his jeans, widening the hole above his knee.

"Let's get it on here," he said, glancing up.

"Here? What about people?"

"It's early. No one's home."

I twisted in my seat and looked around. The street was lined with timid maples. Nothing was moving.

"You lie down in the back seat first and get settled. Then I'll climb on top of you," Stephen said.

This wasn't at all what I'd planned on but we'd come this far, we might as well get something out of it.

The back seat was so tiny, I was barely able to squeeze in. I bent my knees and pressed my feet up against the side window. Stephen was over six feet tall. He'd never fit.

"This isn't going to work," I called out.

Stephen didn't reply. He tucked his limbs in, like he was made of hinged pick-up sticks, hunched over and wiggled into the back. His head bonked the ceiling. His elbow poked me in the eye.

"Watch it!"

"Just hang on a minute," he said.

His knees were almost up by his shoulders as he positioned himself on top of me. He pressed one hand against the rear window to steady himself. The other hand unbuttoned his fly.

"Ow," I said when he entered. This wasn't working.

"It will feel good in a minute."

I tried to relax. *It will*, I thought. *It usually does.*

Then I looked up and saw a boy, about eight years old, wearing a striped red and white T-shirt, standing near the side window. His hair was shaved close to his head, like a marine. He clasped a large blue beach ball to his chest. His face was set in the solemn expression children have when they listen to ghost stories. I wanted to shoo him away but I was pinned.

*What could he see?* Just Stephen's skinny backside bobbing up and down and the soles of my shoes squashed against the glass. I felt a zap of fear. *Was the boy going to dart home and tell his parents?* But he didn't move. He just stood there, a few feet away, staring. I imagined how we must look from the street, how desperate and ludicrous.

Finally, the boy turned and threw the ball a few feet. It bounced high off the sidewalk. He dashed after it, grabbed it and kept on going. I wanted to shove Stephen off of me and run away, too.

Circe was trotting down the hall, almost to the living room, when we came in after dark, my favorite Jefferson Airplane album, *Surrealistic Pillow*, snared between her teeth. Her head was high, her back straight, the look of a dog with a purpose. When she saw me, her ears flattened and the album fell from her mouth. She dropped to her belly and dragged her body toward me.

I squatted down and tried to sound stern.

"What did you do?"

She crawled closer.

"Check this out," Stephen said, pointing to a pile of my albums under the bay window in the living room.

The picture of Jacqueline Du Pre's face was gone. Only her cello was visible over the gummy cardboard. Both Bob Dylan and the girl beside him on the wintery Greenwich Village street had been digested. I pulled the record out of its soggy sleeve. It was punctured with teeth marks.

"God, she's ruined all of them. She must have been working on this for hours," I said.

I turned toward my dog.

"Circe!"

She rolled on her back, legs up, belly exposed. Her tail scraped a dirge along the floor.

"Bad dog," I said, without conviction.

I couldn't be mad. She was so contrite. Besides, I should never have left her behind. I should have been out at the ocean throwing her Frisbee instead of contorted in the back seat of my car. We both would have been happier.

# 18

By January, five months after Stephen broke into my apartment, my resentment grew with every bag of groceries I carried up the walk. *Freeloader*—a word I'd never used, one that belonged to my father's generation—began to glow like neon in my mind, bright and green and blinking. Stephen must have sensed my irritation because one evening I came home to find his eyes clear and the classified ad section of *The San Francisco Chronicle* spread out in front of him on the kitchen table. Days later, he called me at the lumber company to tell me the good news—he'd landed a job painting houses starting the following Monday. When I walked in that night, he was waiting, dressed in white overalls and a jaunty matching cap the company had provided. He spun around so I could admire his uniform, an eager expression on his face, like a boy ready to go trick-or-treating.

Every morning the next week, another painter picked Stephen up and I drove to the lumber company where my secretarial duties rarely varied. But knowing that Stephen was working as well made fetching Mr. O'Connor another cup of coffee more bearable. That good feeling lasted for five days. When I came home on Friday, Stephen was already stretched out in my bed, the nub of a joint crackling between his fingers.

"What happened?" I stopped a few feet from him.

"The jerk fired me," Stephen said, staring at the ceiling, his chin jutting out defiantly.

"Why? You showed up every day, didn't you?"

"Yeah. But he said I was too slow. I wasn't getting enough done."

A bell chimed in my head.

"You weren't high during the day, were you?"

"Of course. Are you crazy? Do you have any idea how boring painting is?" He took a deep toke, snickered, coughed, then turned toward me. "I don't care. I hated that job. Stupid waste of time."

He held out the joint but I shook my head.

"What are you going to do all day? Just stay stoned?"

"What's wrong with that?" His upper lip twitched.

"What are you going to do for money?"

"When my weed runs out, I can always get a few odd jobs. Maybe sell some grass."

I didn't have any response. I felt too exhausted and empty.

After that, Stephen went back to waiting for me at my apartment or dropping by in the evening. Occasionally, he'd mention seeing someone from The Orange Zucchinis. The band and their entourage had been rooming in different locales around Marin, and Stephen hitchhiked or rode the bus to visit. I knew he sometimes got together with one of the members of the band to buy grass, and that he kept up with Bonnie, the pale blond woman I first saw at his side. He said she was back on welfare with the toddler Stephen claimed wasn't his, and she'd completed a week of training in EST, a hodge-podge philosophy combining Zen with humiliation.

One evening, as I lay next to him after sex, he seemed calmer than usual. Suddenly, I realized why.

"Do you go see Bonnie while I'm at work?"

"Sure. She needs some loving, too."

"But you're with me now. That's not right."

"She's just a poor woman. No different than you. You don't

want to deny her some affection, do you? It's not like there isn't enough for you."

He had me there.

We didn't talk about her again. Oddly, I wasn't jealous. I observed my numbness with an almost scientific detachment, aware how much Stephen's hold on me was loosening.

By February, he was waiting for me, high and needy, whimpering for us to climb under the sheets as soon as I came home from work. I'd agree, waiting for the pleasure to roll back in, but after hours of typing invoices in a Quonset hut, having sex with Stephen felt like one more chore.

An image formed and asserted itself in my mind, like a waking dream. Stephen and I are fifty feet down in the ocean in our street clothes, treading water in a kelp forest where so little sunlight cut through, objects are visible only a few feet away. I can't hold my breath any longer. As I try to kick toward the surface, Stephen wraps his fingers around one of my ankles and pulls me back. I reach down to peel off his grip but I can't pry him loose. His hair dances like tentacles around his face. He is smiling. He wants me to drown with him.

On a Saturday afternoon, six months after we first met, we sat across from each other in the living room. It was early March, California winter, the rainy season. Stephen pressed himself against the edge of the couch and I faced him from the mohair chair. Circe lay by my feet.

"This isn't working anymore. You need to move out," I said.

He nodded, not surprised. "Where am I supposed to go?" he said, studying his hands.

"I don't know."

He didn't look up.

"How about with Bonnie and Keith?" I said.

"No. She's in a little place. With two other people. There's no room for me."

His skin looked pale and parched, like an old man's face. His shoulders sagged. I had to get him out before he started to beg and I gave in.

"You'll find someplace. You always do."

# COUNSELOR

# 19

I opened my eyes as the first ring faded and saw Circe lift her head. By the second ring, she leaped off my bed, her tail high, racing toward the front of the apartment. The only phone was on the floor in the living room.

"Jane," I called out toward her room, without getting up. I lifted the alarm clock to my face. It was two-thirty in the morning.

"Jane."

I wasn't sure if she'd come back during the night or was staying at her boyfriend's as she did most of the time now. In any case, the call was probably for her.

The phone was as insistent as a siren. *All right. I'm coming.* I grabbed my robe from the foot of the bed and stuffed my arms into the sleeves. The wooden floor in the hallway was tacky with grime. When was the last time anyone had cleaned around here?

"Hey, it's me. How you doing?" I heard Stephen say when I picked up the receiver. His voice had a tinny sound.

I started to say I'd been asleep, but before I could speak he added, "Listen, I don't have much time."

I hadn't talked to him in eight days, not since he threw his rucksack over his shoulder and ambled out, not since I'd escaped.

I dropped down in the chair. Nearby, Circe knocked her blue rubber ball out from under the couch and bounded into the dining room after it.

"I'm in a little trouble. I could use your help," he said.

I began working through possible replies: *I didn't have any money; it wasn't working out; he needed to fend for himself.* I heard irregular, hard slamming sounds. *Where was he anyway? A pool hall?* The voices in the background sounded urgent, muffled and male.

"I've been arrested. I'm in the police station in San Francisco. It's not too bad, nothing serious."

Circe dropped her ball on my lap. She sat alongside the chair, her tail thumping against the floor, watching me. When I didn't respond, she rested her chin on the padded arm and stared up at me, her black eyes hopeful.

"What happened?" I asked, certain I already knew.

I imagined Stephen on a narrow street in San Rafael, wearing his denim jacket, the collar turned up for warmth. I saw him slink beside a large house, slide open a window, drop one leg over the side, climb in, then, in the dark, grope around until he found a chair. I remembered what he told me the week we'd met when I asked about burglary. "For me, it's very sexual, like violating a woman, getting inside her. When I broke into someone's home, I used to sit there for a while, enjoying the rush, before I took anything."

Tonight he must have picked the wrong house.

He cleared his throat. "You won't like this. I can explain it to you when I see you." It was hard to make out his words. Maybe the connection was bad.

"What? Is someone injured? Are you hurt?"

"No. Nothing like that. I jumped a woman and got busted, that's all. Do you think you can help me?"

"What?" I was having trouble holding onto the pieces.

"I need your help."

"What are you saying?"

His voice grew faint. "I'm almost done. Just give me another minute. I'm talking to my old lady." Then louder. "The cop was signaling me. I've used up my time. There's a line of guys behind me. Listen, if you could come by tomorrow, they'll release me on bail. You'll need five hundred dollars."

"Five hundred dollars. I don't have that."

"Can't you borrow it? I'll pay it back. I swear to you. I won't let you down."

His voice picked up speed and for the first time, as it rose and thinned out, I heard the fear.

"I don't understand. Who was the woman?"

"I just scared her. I didn't hurt her. I know how you feel about something like this. But there's no one else I could ask."

"Why don't you call Bonnie?" She had been with him— what?—ten years or so. She must have bailed him out in all that time.

"Bonnie? Bonnie will be useless. She can barely dress herself. I need your help. Please. You're the only one I can turn to."

Suddenly, everything stopped.

*You're the only one I can turn to.*

The voice, flickering on the line, had the same parched quality as my father's the night I sat beside him on my parents' bed and he begged me not to leave him.

*Don't think that way,* I told myself. *This is your chance to get away. Look at what he did. He attacked a woman. You don't protect would-be rapists. Tell him that, say no.*

But another female voice, one with authority and enough resonance to fill a concert hall, pushed in. *You can't abandon a man when he needs you. You have to help him.* The voice overtook mine and smothered it. *He's my own, my wounded, my boy,* it said. And then, with towering ferocity added, *Nothing will block my way.*

Three months later, the woman Stephen had assaulted ambled to her seat in the front of the almost empty courtroom, as relaxed as if she'd come to a theater and there was plenty of time before the show. She was in her mid-twenties, my age, with springy brown curls that wound down her back. A big floppy tapestry purse with drawstrings hung over her shoulder. She wore a denim skirt, white blouse and black boots. I hadn't known what to expect, but I'd never imagined she'd look like me.

After a few moments, she turned in her seat, glancing past Stephen with his head drooped down, and scanned our side of the room. Her gaze found me, as though she knew I'd be there. Then she nodded and smiled, the look one woman gives another that says *life is tough, men are jerks, and I understand just what you're going through*. I worked to meet her eyes, stunned by her generosity, and tried to smile back. It was all I could do to paste that lie on my face.

When I'd hired a local lawyer, a huge hulk of a man, he'd been confident he could win a light sentence for Stephen, if not get him released altogether. The lawyer had strutted around his small office, hands resting lightly across his big stomach. He explained he'd have to take the woman apart on the stand, ask what kind of underwear she was wearing that night, how often she'd had sex, things like that. Since Stephen had a rap sheet, his defense would be to make both parties look like sleaze. It was ugly stuff, he said, but that's what was needed. Could I handle it? Yes, whatever it took, I'd replied, tasting chalk in my mouth at such a massive betrayal of another woman.

Now, in the courtroom, the judge, a man with the pointy teeth of a ferret, lifted papers affixed to a clipboard and read the charges: assault and battery, attempted rape, the short version of what Stephen had told me the morning I posted his bail.

He'd been standing on the side of the road, hitchhiking, about nine at night, in the north corner of San Francisco, the last neighborhood before the tree-lined road widened and sped to the Golden Gate Bridge. Across the way, a car pulled to the curb and a woman climbed out, the kind of woman he knew he could easily get into bed. After the car drove away, she crossed to his side and gave him a little smile as she strolled past. He was preparing to come on to her when something clicked in his mind and, with all the traffic racing by, charged after her, knocked her down, dragged her back into some bushes, yanked up her skirt and tried to rape her. She pushed him off, ran and started screaming. Stephen dashed around the corner and dove under a parked car, but he didn't stay there. He crawled out from under the chassis and started running along the street.

The overhead light in the courtroom made everyone look sallow. The judge flipped another page on his clipboard and read Stephen's prior crimes aloud. Stephen was already slumped down in his seat, but with each offence he slid further, until his head was barely visible over the top of the chair. The judge asked if there was anything else the court should know before ruling. I stopped breathing, bracing myself for what was coming next: the defense lawyer's attempt to take the victim apart on the witness stand. Instead, the lawyer rose as if his knees hurt, his black suit jacket straining across his massive back, and in a pleading tone requested a light sentence since no harm was done. The judge stared at him, at all of us. His mouth puckered. Then he slammed down his gavel and said: Three to five years in prison, report to the courthouse in two months, released on bail until then.

# 20

The next two months played out in dim grey. I reported to work at the lumber company each day as though nothing had changed, then on weekends drove down to San Francisco, to an old Italian neighborhood where Stephen now resided in a flophouse of a hotel. Jane had already been spending most of her time at her boyfriend's and, not long after the trial, she moved in with him. I couldn't afford to stay on in our Victorian flat by myself and didn't have the energy to look for people to share the rent. Instead, I answered an ad for a roommate in an unfurnished little house farther out in Marin, just blocks from the park where Circe had chased Frisbees. I moved in a few days before Stephen was scheduled to go to prison.

On his last night of freedom Stephen joined me there. We walked through empty rooms like ghosts, avoiding contact and speech. In the dining room, I'd set out two tired bentwood chairs and a Chinese lamp table, giving us a place to eat. Along one wall, a stack of boxes with my books sat over the heater vent. Above them, on the wall, I'd nailed a frayed green and red Caucasian rug I'd found in a thrift store. It had seemed crazy to hang it when so much of what I owned was still in cartons, but it helped make the house feel less desolate.

It was late August, maybe sixty degrees outside, but I couldn't get warm. I burrowed into a box with the word "clothes" scrawled in black Magic Marker on the cardboard and pulled out a red sweater. Circe stayed close to my feet. I went into the kitchen to feed her and she followed, nuzzling my hand. When she bent her head to eat, her white tail waved high and slow in the air, like someone signaling a truce.

Stephen lit another joint and passed it to me. I pulled the smoke in but there was no heat, just the taste of ash.

"We should probably get some sleep. I need to report in early tomorrow," he said.

*People do this*, I thought. *People show up for incarceration.* Their lovers drive them to the county jail and kiss them good-bye, like enlisted men reporting for duty. Except they're going off to cages in a state prison. *If it were me, I'd run.*

Stephen said he had fled. He'd run to the police.

"I could have escaped," he told me when he was out on bail. "After the woman got away, I hid under some cars. I heard sirens and realized the cops were driving right by. They'd never find me. So I climbed out and ran along the street."

When I asked him why, he said he was out of options.

"I knew you wouldn't take me back. I was going down. Prison seemed like a safe place. It's hard, but if you know how to act, it can be all right."

There was an old thermostat on the wall near the kitchen. I turned it up to eighty and heard something thump under the floorboards. I stood by the vent, hoping for heat, but there was no warmth yet from the small blue gas flames ignited ten feet below.

Circe always slept on the floor near me but not this night. I heard her nails clicking on the floor as she wandered into the adjoining empty bedroom, the one my new roommate would move into later this week. It was almost midnight when I entered my room, not much bigger than a cell, lay down next to Stephen in bed and pulled the blanket over us. The heat from the furnace was just starting to kick in as I fell asleep.

Hours later, hot air blasted me awake.

*I must have overdone it. I'll turn the thermostat down.*

I opened my eyes and saw colors—gold and red and orange. The wall in front of me, the doorway out, had been devoured, replaced by a mural of flames.

"Stephen, wake up," He lay on his back, his mouth open. I shook his shoulder. "The house is on fire. We have to get out."

Stephen sat up beside me, oddly still, while the inferno roared at our feet. *What to do?* Above my head was a window. I slid one glass panel over the other and started to pull myself out. Then I remembered to grab the sheet. I didn't want to be standing in the street naked. Stephen followed, wrapping the blanket around his waist.

Behind us the house was a wall of sparkling light, crunching, crackling, ripping. The wooden siding, the front door, the roof peeled off as we watched from the sidewalk. The layers were like sheets of paper, ripped away in the wind.

People from the neighborhood surrounded us but no one stood too close. They talked softly to each other. One man said, "It was like a tinderbox. I saw a small flame, then just like that"—he snapped his fingers—"it went up."

There were houses on either side of ours. An arm of fire reached out toward the asphalt roof of one but didn't grab on. I knew it wouldn't. The people who lived there had done nothing wrong.

No one spoke to me. I didn't want them to. They were strangers. All I could do was hold the sheet tight around me, watch the fire and wait for my dog to find me.

"Circe!" I shouted every few seconds.

She would be all right. A dog who dove off piers would find a way out. A dog who stopped traffic with a Frisbee could dart through flames.

The sirens carved out a path with their screams. Firemen with heavy boots pushed past us. They looked like the firefighters in all the children's books I'd ever read. After their hoses smothered the blaze, three firemen stopped nearby. I turned to the youngest, a man a little older than me.

"Did you see my dog?" I asked. "She's a white German shepherd." His face was black with ash.

"No," he said. "I didn't. She probably got scared and ran away. She'll come back."

Before I could shout her name again, a fireman as old as my father stepped out from behind the first.

"Your dog is dead," he said. "We found her body. She died from the smoke."

The concrete walkway dissolved beneath my feet along with the sense of the boundaries of my body. I couldn't stop crying. A neighbor touched my elbow and steered me into her house. Stephen shuffled beside me. Inside, I lifted the heavy receiver on the telephone and dialed Paul, the only person I could think of who could help.

His wife answered, barely awake, and when she put Paul on, I said, "Everything's gone. Circe's dead. The house burned down. Come get me."

The next morning I phoned the police station and described what had happened. They granted Stephen four more hours of freedom. For once, there was something Stephen could do for me. He and Paul would bury Circe in the backyard where the fire never reached.

When the time came, I handed Paul her Frisbee and a blue rubber ball from the trunk of my car so they could put her toys down with her. They wrapped her in the blanket that had covered Stephen the night before. I couldn't bring myself to look at her, my sweet friend, my athlete. Later, Paul told me her body wasn't really burned. I wanted to believe she hadn't suffered, that she didn't wake up at all.

## 21

I t took three months to finish with Stephen. In the beginning, I drove an hour and a half every Saturday to the prison at Vacaville, a working-class town northeast of San Francisco, and sat across from him at a small table in a huge room that looked like a cafeteria. All around us, at tables of their own, other denim-clad inmates huddled close to their visitors, mostly women with heavy makeup and subdued children. I'd been surprised to see that the prison allowed convicts to have meetings like this. In movies, they were always constrained behind a glass wall. A few times I saw Timothy Leary, a man I recognized from the newspapers, the former Harvard instructor famous for promoting LSD. He was tanned and smiling, as relaxed as if he were in a country club, regaling a table full of captivated young men and women.

I never announced my exit nor consciously planned it, but gradually Stephen's hold on me weakened until it lost its grip entirely. It was much harder to finish mourning for my dog. I was sure I'd caused the fire, not only because I'd left a book box on a vent and turned on the heat, but because of how I'd been living. My guilt and grief were relentless, but there was no place for emotion in the Quonset hut at the lumber company or in the dust-filled house where I'd rented a room. So late at night I'd climb into my VW Beetle, roll up the windows and drive along empty streets, keening until I felt too drained to cry anymore.

Karate pulled me through. During the ten months I'd known Stephen, I'd gone to class occasionally, but gradually I went back to training three or four times a week. The other students and teachers kidded me in the same comforting high school locker-room way they always had. No one asked questions.

I resumed stretching and lifting weights. That combination used to be all anyone did to enhance their performance, but in the time I'd been away some of the top students had begun running for endurance. Now I was determined to add running to my regime as well so I wouldn't be left behind.

The track at the junior college was abandoned on a cold Saturday afternoon in March 1974. Fog smoked across the surrounding lawn and lay against the empty bleachers. It was hard to believe that a lap was only a quarter of a mile. I could make it only halfway around before I had to stop, brace my hands on my knees, and suck in air.

I'd never been much of a runner. When I could breathe evenly I started up again, hearing the soles of my sneakers smack the packed dirt and feeling the impact shoot into my shins. This time I made it three-fourths of the way around before a spasm started in my side. That was enough for one day. I turned toward the gate, heading to the parking lot.

"You can do better than that," a male voice shouted.

I flinched. I thought I'd been alone. On the other side of the track, up in the bleachers, I could make out a dark shape, a form in a hooded sweatshirt, but I couldn't see the features.

*Great. Just what I need. Some jerk showing up to heckle me.* Without thinking, I shifted into a neutral fighting stance.

"You're just going too fast," the voice called out. "Slow it down." The tone was friendly.

I watched the man as he rose and jogged down the bleacher steps, moving toward me. As he got closer the tension left my body. It was Lee, one of the brown belts from our sister school.

For the past few months he'd started showing up at our dojo on Saturdays, often pairing up with me during class. We'd barely spoken off the mat because as soon as the session ended, he'd grab his knapsack and dart out the door.

"What are you doing here?" I said.

"I heard you say you were coming over here. I thought you might need a little encouragement."

He stopped a few feet from me, waiting, his eyebrows raised slightly, a tentative smile on his face. His kindness surprised me. I smiled back.

"Do you know how anyone can run for miles? It doesn't seem possible," I said.

His face relaxed. He untied the strings under his hood and yanked it off his head. For a moment I flashed on the first time I'd seen him. It had been a few years earlier, at a martial arts tournament in the hot central valley, and he was sparring with a much larger opponent. Lee had been an odd sight. With a stringy beard, fogged-over, wire-rim glasses, and a long ponytail brushing the top of his purple belt, he'd looked like a Rumpelstiltskin—the quirky sidekick in the story, not the leading man. Now his glasses had been replaced by contact lenses. His hair was short and fit his head like a cap. His beard was trim and shaped to his jaw. He had even features, high cheekbones—really a handsome face. It was hard to believe this was the same person.

"I ran track in high school. You've got to pace yourself. You can't get far if you start out sprinting," he said.

I'd never considered that. I could vary the speed. Lee climbed back into the bleachers and I started running again, but this time I didn't go full out.

"Looking good," he yelled.

I could just make out his outline against the white sky.

As I rounded the far corner, he called out, "Take it easier. You don't have to push that hard."

Over the next six months, Lee began showing up Tuesdays and Thursdays at my karate school for the advanced class, and I was glad to see him. He was the only student who was willing to pair up with me. The rest of the men didn't want to work out with a small woman, and I didn't blame them. I'd rather be challenged by someone stronger as well.

But Lee was always willing to help me train. When I couldn't remember the next move from *Monkey Steals the Peach* or *Mongoose Bites the Cobra*, he'd rise from a stretch, wipe his hands on his *gi* bottoms, then pantomime the self-defense sequence. Other times, he'd strap on padded gloves that looked like flattened catcher's mitts, glide backward around the mat and hold these paws out at different angles while I nailed them with kicks and punches. Unlike other men in class who had to partner with me on occasion, Lee didn't weaken his grip or, going to the other extreme, try to shatter my kneecaps. He matched my spirit, coming back at me hard when I went full force, going half-speed when I asked. With him I was a worthy opponent, nothing more.

At least on the mat. He never explained why he was so accommodating and I didn't ask. I assumed he had a crush on me from his expression when I'd walk into the dojo, a mopey gaze full of longing. But I didn't want to know. He never came on to me and I was relieved.

Lee and I rarely trained outdoors but one humid afternoon in July, when the dojo seemed to be extruding heat, I suggested we finish our workout by my apartment. I'd recently found a studio in a converted Victorian house just a few minutes' drive from the karate school. There wasn't any need for either of us to warm up again. After parking in the front, I resumed my forms. Lee stood in my driveway and went back to practicing his jumping spinning kick. When I'd finished my *katas*, I plunked down on the little strip of lawn next to my building to take a break and watch.

Just as he'd been doing for the past twenty minutes, Lee dropped into a fighting stance and shifted his weight over the balls of his feet. The lines in his forehead deepened, his eyes narrowed and his expression changed into one I'd seen many times during the months we'd trained together—a combination of concentration and something like sorrow.

Then he leaped straight up, rising several feet off the concrete. As he ascended, his body whipped around ninety degrees and, at the top of his rise, his rear leg snapped out. The kick retracted as fast as it extended, the momentum rotating him around in the air. He landed exactly where he started, on the ground, fists clenched, ready to fight.

"Looks good," I said, standing and wiping some grass off the back of my karate pants. Lee nodded but didn't answer. He was readying himself for his next jump.

I never expected to do this flying kick well, just well enough to pass my upcoming brown belt test. Since *kenpo* was a fighting style, not an acrobatic one, the head of our karate association only needed to see a reasonable approximation of this novelty move.

I rose, shook my legs to get some blood flowing, and started to throw combinations of kicks. A man strolling by noticed us, then paused. I stopped but Lee ignored him and continued practicing. The man was thin like a Russian wolfhound and expensive-looking. He wore fashionable glasses and was tall, six foot two or more. It was hard to gauge. He stood just off to the side, his legs wide apart as though he were straddling a horse, arms crossed over his chest. He watched Lee execute the flying spinning kick several times before he spoke.

"What could you ever do with a kick like that?"

Lee squinted up at the man as if seeing him through a haze, and wiggled his finger for him to come closer. The man strode forward, smirking, clearly delighted by the entertainment. Lee pointed to a spot on the sidewalk, three feet in front of him, and the man walked to it.

"Stand still," Lee said in a low, tense voice.

Lee dropped into a bow stance, bending his knees lower than before, his back straight. Beads of sweat slid down his cheeks. He shifted his weight slightly, centering himself. Then he flew straight up, whipping his leg around. In mid-air, his foot snared the edge of the man's glasses, ripping them off his face and hurling them through the air. They landed near the side of the house about ten feet away, hiding in the dirt among some spent lilacs.

Lee landed in stance directly in front of the man, hands cocked into fists alongside his head, protecting his face like a boxer.

"That's what that kick is good for," Lee said, almost in a whisper.

The man rushed to find his glasses, kneeling in front of the plants and feeling around for the frames.

"I see. I see," he said as he seated his glasses back on his face.

When he rose, he seemed to bow slightly to Lee, or at least he bobbed up and down. He backed away, facing us, and didn't turn to look where he was going until he was a few car lengths away. Then he almost broke into a jog.

Lee didn't stop, didn't smile, didn't even glance after the man. He readied himself for his next kick as though nothing had happened. *Okay. If he wasn't going to say anything, I wasn't about to either.* I went back to training, launching combinations of punches, but inside I was doing cartwheels. My training partner was a karate William Tell!

I felt almost as proud as if I'd thrown that kick myself.

# 22

I left the lumber company and got another secretarial job at a lamp distributor, but I never fit in. The other clerical worker was happy to stay after-hours when asked, but I refused, confident that a few extra dollars couldn't compensate for lost karate time. After my boss fired me, saying I should never take that kind of work again, I realized she was right. In fact, she'd done me a favor. I was twenty-five. It was time to get serious about what I wanted to do and that was to be a counselor, to help people heal.

It took a while, but eventually I got a job as a live-in residential counselor with a company that ran group homes for teenage boys. I'd be working solo shifts that alternated between twenty-four and forty-eight hours. The boys in the home had come under the auspices of one of two agencies, either the police for petty crimes like car theft, or social services because no one wanted them.

It was almost as if I were fated to find this job. A few weeks before I was hired, I'd sold my latest tired VW bug and purchased a ten-year-old 350 Ford Econoline van with low mileage. Except for the driver and passenger seats, the interior was an open shell. It had belonged to a commercial cleaning company, Smithers Mobile Janitorial Service, whose name and phone number were still painted in large red letters on the sides. The van rattled. The advertising looked tacky. But it was the perfect vehicle for my new work. When we went on outings, I could cram all the kids inside.

On my first day at the group home, three hours after my supervisor had left me alone for my first two-day shift, I sat at the head of a long dining room table.

"You know anything about working with boys?" an eighteen-year-old with cold blue eyes called out, tipping back in his chair and glaring at me from the other side of the table. Seven other teenage male faces followed his gaze and stared at me.

"Why are you here?" a boy the size of a linebacker yelled from the other end of the table. He wore a black leather jacket, a few shades darker than his face.

"Yeah, couldn't you get a better job? You must really be desperate," a young boy in a sock cap said, and laughed.

I'd singled out this little boy with basset-hound eyes and toffee colored skin earlier, happy to find anyone shorter than I was.

I offered the same response I'd used at my interview, when the president of the group home asked about my qualifications.

"I really like working as a counselor. It's what I did at my last job. I enjoy helping kids."

I didn't tell the president I had only been in the other group home for two months, working the graveyard shift and checking on three sleeping children, ages eight to twelve. I pointed out my bachelor's degree without mentioning I'd majored in art. And I described selling secondhand goods I scrounged at yard sales as supporting myself through college, which was true, but just barely. My mother's checks every month really did that. I omitted my six weeks as the cleaning lady of a San Francisco synagogue where the head of the sisterhood fired me after she caught me smoking a cigar in the temple kitchen. And I skipped O'Connor Lumber Company and the subsequent part-time clerical jobs I held after Stephen went to prison.

No one asked, so no one needed to know that this was the first job I'd held involving any responsibility for other people. There was also no reason to mention how much I wished this position, the only one to come along, had been with girls instead. Packs of teenage boys had always scared me, the way they circled like hyenas.

It was only my martial arts training that gave me the confidence to take this on.

"This is really an ideal job for me," I told the boys around the dinner table. "I like working these shifts because I can train in karate on my days off. Anyone here know anything about ka-ra-te?"

I elongated the word because I wanted to get their attention. Glancing around, realizing everyone had stopped slurping their spaghetti, I saw that I had.

"I've been training in *kenpo* karate for years. I even teach a few classes. If you guys like, I could show you some moves tomorrow."

One pale boy who seemed sedated looked up. He'd been staring into a crater he'd carved out in the center of his dinner.

"Could be cool," he said slowly.

"Karate? Like Bruce Lee?" another boy said. He was small and delicate, with almond-shaped eyes and skin the color of amber. It was the first time he'd spoken since I'd arrived.

"Something like that. Different style, though."

"Wow," he said. "The Great Nina."

I scanned his face, ready for some sarcastic remark, but he met my gaze with a shy, hopeful smile. He wasn't joking; he really meant it.

"Not quite," I replied, suddenly uncomfortable.

I'd never spent time in this part of San Francisco before, a residential neighborhood near the ocean of sturdy, two-story stucco houses painted neutral colors that blended into shades of gray in the fog. Each property seemed to be allotted the same amount of space, with the same size front yard marked off by an occasional fence. There were no children running down the street, no litter blowing along the sidewalk. It was an ordinary community, the perfect place to hide a facility for problem boys.

After finishing dinner and supervising cleanup, I wandered through the house, not sure what I was supposed to do. The rooms were filled with smells I hadn't encountered since childhood, reminding me of bowls encrusted with Chef Boyardee ravioli, wadded-up socks in my brother's bedroom and damp concrete from the public bathrooms at Jones Beach.

I strolled into the living room where some of the boys had gathered. An old black-and-white TV with a cracked plastic top was tuned to a game show. Earlier in the day, when the supervisor had introduced me to each resident, I'd said hello and repeated their names, trying to stick the information on a mental corkboard alongside their photo. But I'd already forgotten most of them. Now I looked over at the three boys sitting on a worn tweed couch. One, a wiry boy who hadn't spoken during the meal, dangled his feet off a vinyl ottoman. His skin had the sheen of wax fruit. The smallest boy, the one with the sock cap, burrowed into the far corner. The sedated boy sank in the center, his arms slack by his sides, his head tilted straight back up, facing the ceiling.

I pulled over a dining room chair and sat down.

"What are you guys watching?" I asked.

"Dunno," the sedated boy muttered.

"I think these games shows are all rigged. How about you?" I said.

"Who cares," the little one said, dragging his sock cap lower on his forehead as though that stopped me from seeing him.

The eighteen-year-old with cold blue eyes strode out of the kitchen.

"Are you still going through with it?" he asked the room in general.

The boy with waxy skin bobbed his head up and down. "Oh yeah," he said.

"Everyone in this house is so juvenile," the eighteen-year-old said. "Why don't you all just grow up?"

"What's going on?" I asked.

"Nothing," the older boy said and bounded upstairs.

Last week's champion was losing. The game show host told him it wasn't too late to stage a comeback. The show's background music grew louder, a metronome-tight beat played by scratchy horns. The upstairs toilet flushed.

Someone yelled, "Shut the goddam door—that stinks."

I looked at the boys on the couch. The sedated boy's hair was clumped together. *When was the last time he bathed?* The room felt airless and oppressive. It was hard to believe I'd only been here for six hours, that this was still my first day. I needed to move around.

I rose and turned toward the kitchen. As I did, the linebacker appeared and stood like a wall before me. He wore the same black leather jacket he had on all day. I started to step around him but he grinned, leaned over and grabbed me, scooping me up off the ground and pressing me against his huge chest.

"I've got her," he said, pivoting around so everyone could see his catch. "I sure got her."

*What was he planning to do?*

I flashed on an image of being dunked in the bathtub upstairs, clothes on, a clump of boys cheering from the doorway.

"Yeah. You proved you are big and strong. Now put me down."

The boy with the waxy skin sprang from the sofa and darted behind the linebacker. The huge boy had stopped grinning. The leather on his sleeves stuck to my arms.

All the boys hooted.

They knew this was going to happen. No one was going to lift a hand to help me. This wasn't just one clown showing off for the crowd. *Stay calm.* I shifted my weight and the linebacker tightened his grip. There was no way I could twist free. A muscle spasmed in my neck. *They're hoping you'll flail around. They want a spectacle. Don't give it to them.*

One of the first things my karate teacher taught me was never to struggle. He said, "You are too small to overpower someone. So if you can't break a hold right away, wait for an opening. At some point your opponent will think he has you. He'll drop his guard. That's when you counter or run."

The waxy boy led the way to the counselor's office and held the door open as the linebacker ducked under the jamb and strode in, clutching me to his chest. Behind me, the light went on and I heard the deadbolt click.

The counselor's office was not much bigger than a walk-in closet. It held a small desk, two side chairs and a sagging twin-sized bed. The linebacker dropped me in the middle of the bed and lowered himself close beside me.

"You're trapped," he said. His voice had changed. It was deeper, slower, a man's voice.

"Yeah, you can't get away," the waxy boy said. He stood a few feet in front of me, shifting his weight from one foot to the other.

"What are you going to do? We've got you," the linebacker said, leaning close. The folds in his jacket creaked. Balls of sweat dotted his upper lip and forehead.

It felt like a tourniquet was tightening around my ribs.

*Don't show fear.* I worked out a quick strategy. *Get your back to the door and nail them with kicks. Don't let them surround you.*

Maybe I couldn't escape but I knew I could hurt them.

For what seemed like a long time, no one moved. Maybe this was just a test. The lights were still on and so were all the clothes. They probably wanted to see if they could make the new woman counselor squirm.

I turned to look into the linebacker's eyes, trying to hold my gaze. He glared back. I clamped my jaw tight and continued to stare. In less than a minute, he blinked and glanced down. When he tried to look up, he couldn't.

Now I was almost sure he was bluffing.

I stretched my arms out, yawned, and said in a flat, bored voice, "I'm really scared."

*Were they buying this?*

"You're cornered. There's no escape," the linebacker said, his voice in a higher register. He glanced around the tiny room as if he wasn't sure this was still true.

"Right. I'm really frightened. Look." I lifted my hand, holding it steady a foot from my heart. "See. I'm shaking. Now open the door."

*I was going to carry this off!*

The two teenagers looked at each other.

"You can't get away," the waxy boy said, but his voice cracked.

"Yeah. Sure. Unlock the door."

*Time to make my move.*

I rose, put my hands on my hips, my back to the desk and faced them.

The linebacker's large frame seemed to collapse. He hunched down, dropping his head, wrapping his arms around his chest, rocking back and forth. When he lifted his face, he had the expression of a naughty little boy, irresistible to any mother.

The waxy boy slid a few feet away from me and stuffed his hands in his pockets. He kicked one heel of his sneakers against the other like he was knocking the mud off his shoes before coming inside the house. A good boy.

"We were only kidding," the linebacker said. "We didn't mean anything."

"I know. It's all right," I said.

*I'm all right.*

I unlocked the door. The living room was filled with boys. It looked like all of them had crammed in and were waiting. As I emerged from the office, everyone stopped moving, as though they were playing the kids' game where the leader calls out "Freeze."

I walked over to the vinyl ottoman and sat down in front of the TV, trying to seem relaxed. In an instant, the boys came to life. The little one with the sock hat bopped the sedated boy in the head with a bolster.

"Asshole," the sedated boy said, but he was grinning. They all were.

The game show on TV was almost over. I recognized the contestant. It was last week's champion. Apparently he was still in the game.

# TRAINING PARTNER

# 23

Three boys became my favorites: Percil, with the sock cap, Barry, who seemed sedated but wasn't, more likely clinically depressed, and shy Mark, who'd called me "the Great Nina." These boys were all small, pretended to be tough and had no one at home to protect them. They were the ones most like me.

I wasn't supposed to prefer any but it was impossible to meet the demands of eight urgent teenagers. Besides, most of the bigger boys could fend for themselves. I'd formed a plan to stay on for three years, to see the boys I cared most about through to their emancipation. But after working there for six months, I knew my timeline was a fantasy. I'd be lucky to make it through a year.

One Friday afternoon, in my tenth month at the group home and an hour into my shift, I sat in the office, staring at a picture of the thigh bone in an anatomy book I was studying for an upcoming brown belt test. A drawing showed the femur, the longest, strongest bone in the body, the bone that the ape-man hurled into the air at the beginning of *2001: A Space Odyssey*. I'd been counting on a little time to myself when I heard a knock.

"It's open," I said.

Percil pushed the door ajar. His jeans were gathered around his waist with a belt and rolled up at the bottoms to fit his small frame. He had on the same blue wool sock cap he always wore.

"You might want to know... " Percil said, stretching out his words as he leaned against the doorframe. "Calvin has a girl in the basement."

"I'll tell her to leave in a little while."

Girls weren't allowed in the house without the counselor's permission, but what difference could a few minutes make? I glanced back down at my diagram.

*There are two trochanters: the greater and the lesser.*

He shifted his weight.

"Yeah, well, he's screwing her," he said.

My eyelid started twitching before I'd gotten to my feet. The other two boys I liked best, Mark and Barry, must have known about this already because they were standing in the dining room, huddled together, whispering excitedly as I dashed past. They fell in behind Percil, who strode two feet behind me.

"Wait here," I told the procession as I opened the door to the basement.

I flipped on the light over the stairs, and the single bare bulb lit the gray concrete wall. I descended two steps, then stopped. It was completely quiet.

"Calvin," I called down toward the reserve boxes of cereal and cartons of toilet paper. "You down here, Calvin?"

No answer.

*Maybe Percil was wrong.*

But when I reached the floor, switched on the fluorescent light and turned the corner, there he was—on an old couch, his underwear and pants wrapped around his ankles, his bony white butt in the air, the edges of a girl sprawled beneath him.

I stopped twenty feet away. "Calvin. You're busted."

He kept humping. I didn't want to come any nearer, didn't want to breathe in their acrid smells, but I knew he'd keep ignoring me unless I got up close.

"Calvin. Get off the girl. Pull up your pants. Do it!" I said, now only a few feet away.

He rolled over and they both sat up, yanking at zippers.

Calvin looked at me for the first time, angling his head and flashing his doofus smile. The girl didn't glance up. Her hair was matted to the back of her head, her eyes painted into her face with smudged black liner, the angry-sad look of a group home inmate.

"Calvin, what do you think you're doing?"

He didn't reply and I hadn't expected him to. What I really wanted to ask was: Why now? Why couldn't you have done this earlier when the other counselor was on duty?

They rose, stuffing pieces of loose clothing into their pants, and shuffled to the stairs. I walked a few feet behind. Back in the dining room my three favorite boys were waiting. They followed me, giggling, as I strode to the front door and held it open for the girl, lumpy in her old army coat.

"Don't ever let me see you here again," I said to the girl because that melodramatic line seemed like the kind of thing the counselor was supposed to say.

I turned back to Calvin, his bony arms dangling by his sides.

"You're grounded for a week."

He grinned and bounded up the stairs to the bedrooms, looking more gleeful than I'd ever seen him. I turned to the three watching boys and snapped, "Find something to do with yourselves before dinner," and immediately regretted my tone.

By the time I sat down in the office and stared at the diagram of the thigh bone, the twitch in my eyelid had picked up speed.

The next day went smoothly. Chores were done by noon and in the evening half of the house took the bus to a movie theater on Geary Boulevard. Only my three favorite boys were home, along with Jim, the one with cold blue eyes, the oldest. That was fine; he and I got along well. Curfew wasn't until eleven. I'd have plenty of time to study. I sat at my desk and opened my anatomy book to the section on the lower leg: the tibialis, the fibula and the gastrocnemius.

About twenty minutes later, Barry, the sedated-looking boy, strolled over and leaned against the open doorway.

"Hey," he said.

"Hey." I glanced up at him and smiled.

Barry was dressed in his favorite color, black. Black sneakers, black jeans, black T-shirt with the words "Black Sabbath" in broken, melting silver letters across the front. His face was as pale as if he'd been dipped in flour. He sighed and crossed his arms. He let them drop to his side. He scratched his head. He stuck his hands in his pockets.

"Something up?" I asked.

"Jim's gone off the deep end." Barry put a finger to his mouth and gnawed at what was left of a nail.

Percil, the smallest boy, yelled from the kitchen, "Did you tell her?"

"Tell me what?"

"Out of my way, fool," Percil yelled, pushing past Barry. "Jim is building bombs upstairs. He's going to blow the house up."

A fatigue as numbing as Novocaine snaked through me. I stared down at my textbook, wanting only to focus on the words.

"You got to bust him. Take him to juvie. It's the rules," Percil said, bouncing on the balls of his high-top sneakers.

I looked at Percil. The tiny thirteen-year-old had plenty of energy. Why couldn't he take over for now?

I rose slowly. I was going to have to go upstairs to their rooms, something I rarely did. Percil darted around me as I cut across the living room.

"Jim's going to juvie," he chanted in a singsong voice.

The shy boy and the sedated-looking one, my buddies, followed, clustering behind me as I ascended the stairs and turned into the first bedroom. On the wall, over one of the twin beds, posters of rock musicians in grotesque makeup glared down at me. I caught the wording under one, "Welcome to My Nightmare." Jim was hunched over his desk.

He turned and glanced over. "Oh, I see you brought your little pets."

"What are you doing?" I said.

He slid his chair away from the desk. A pile of wicks, three empty Heinz ketchup bottles, matches and a pyramid of gray powder were assembled in two rows.

"What does it look like? I'm going to blow this fucking place up. I can't stand it anymore." The blue of his eyes seemed iridescent, they were so bright.

Did he really know how to build explosives? It seemed unlikely but I had to act as if he did.

"You know that's wrong, Jim. I'm confiscating all your materials. Give me everything you have now."

He shoved his chair further back, making no attempt to block the desk.

"It's all bullshit. This house, the world," he said, standing, his gaze going dull.

I was relieved at how willing he was to cooperate. He was clearly no threat.

"Come see me downstairs. We need to talk," I said, gathering up his bomb supplies and turning to leave.

My three favorite boys followed me out.

"You've got to take him to juvie," little Percil said, his voice rising.

"I don't think it's necessary."

"No, you've got to. It's the rules. Anything like that. He's got to get busted." Percil grabbed my sleeve.

What would taking him to juvenile hall mean—getting

directions, loading the boys into my van, shouting at them to calm down, driving through San Francisco traffic on a Saturday night, finding a parking spot, waiting to be seen, explaining what Jim had done to some arresting officer, and finally carting the rest of the boys back? By then they'd really be acting crazy. Taking Jim to juvenile hall was the right thing to do, but it was too complicated, too tense, too much.

"It's not appropriate," I said, walking toward the office quickly so I wouldn't have to face them.

I knew I was letting the boys down. They needed clear boundaries and rules. I understood that Jim was terrified of leaving the group home after the semester was over. He and I had been talking about his upcoming emancipation and basic things he'd have to do once he was out in the world, like opening a checking account. He was acting out now, pleading for help. I knew all this but I didn't have the energy to be a hammer.

Back in the office, I stuffed the paper bag with the gunpowder into the bottom desk drawer. I could hear Barry's, Percil's and Mark's voices from the living room, high and agitated, but I couldn't make out their words.

I wanted to shout to them: *I'm locking up the contraband. That's why I'm back in my office. Not because I can't face you. Not because my eyelid won't stop twitching. Not because I'm hiding.*

# 24

The next morning, after cleanup, Mark, the shy boy, sat across from me in the office, hands folded in his lap, watching me with large black eyes. Mine were puffy and red. I'd had a hard time sleeping. Mark smiled at me, waiting to start our counseling session. I tried to give him an encouraging look. I reached around and fumbled in my drawer for a cigarillo, the kind of slender cigar that came with a little yellow plastic pacifier attached to the tip. I'd quit the big stinky stogies years before but had started smoking these recently.

"How's school? Anything new?"

I lit the cigar and cradled the smoke in my mouth.

"Not really."

He gazed at me with a hopeful expression.

"Any more nightmares?"

He looked down and sucked in his lower lip. This must be what he was hoping I'd ask.

"I had the same dream with the green monster chasing me," he said, whispering at the memory.

God, I felt jumpy. I swiveled in my chair, rested the cigar in an ashtray and reached for some sunflower seeds in a bag on my desk. I threw a handful of shells in my mouth, held out the cellophane bag to Mark and jiggled it.

He shook his head no.

I spit the cracked husks into my hand, dropped them in a cereal bowl that was half full of casings, and looked over at Mark. He smiled back wistfully, waiting.

*Didn't he see what a mess I was?*

"What does the monster want?" I asked, trying to sound professional.

"To kill me."

"Why?"

"I don't know." He shrugged.

"If we asked the monster, what would he say?"

I heard a crash, then a chattering sound, like dishes trembling in a cupboard during an earthquake.

"Fucking asshole," a male voice yelled.

"Go fuck yourself," someone snapped back.

My eyelid lurched into spasms.

"Maybe the monster is hungry and he wants to eat me," Mark said.

I held a hand up to silence him. "I've got to see what's going on."

The kitchen was filled with a fetid smell. Jim, the eighteen-year-old bomb-builder, and Dick, sixteen and the newest boy, were standing pressed up to each other, almost chest to chest. Jim's features were twisted with an expression I'd seen before, on the face of a cornered barking dog on a back street in Mexico. Dick's glasses were fogged with the heat from their bodies. The acne on his face was red and raw.

"Don't you call me asshole. You motherfucker."

"Fuck you."

Jim shoved Dick, who stumbled back a foot before lunging in, dropping his shoulder and assuming a tackle position.

Off to the side, the rest of the boys clustered along the wall, transfixed.

*I've got to break this up. I can't have a fight erupt here.*

I hesitated for a second. Both boys were over six feet tall. But I didn't have a choice. I stepped between them, wedged myself in the few inches of space, thrust one hand on each boy's chest and tried to pry them further apart. But they leaned closer together, forcing my arms to bend, acting as if I weren't there.

*These weren't boys. They were bulls.*

For a second I thought they were going to start swinging over my head, pummeling each other with me trapped in the middle.

"That's enough!" I shouted. "Back off. Now."

Neither moved; then Jim stepped away, not taking his eyes off Dick.

It was over. I dropped my arms to my sides. But Dick didn't budge. He towered above me, glaring.

"Don't you tell me what to do, you bitch," he shouted. His spittle sprayed my face.

*Bitch. He called me a bitch.*

I split wide open.

I was fourteen years old, back in my bedroom in Queens, watching my mother as she packed her suitcase, hearing my father bellow as he charged up the stairs, "You're not doing this to me again, you bitch."

*You bitch.*

In that instant, I became my mother, refusing to cower, defiant in the blast. *Don't you dare threaten me.* And I turned into the girl I wish I could have been, not a mute referee, but an avenger.

I grabbed Dick's T-shirt and threw him back so fast, he hit the plaster with a thud. Suddenly, I was my father, boiling over and pouring out the sides, my father, charging at my mother and hurling her against the pink wall. I lunged at Dick and hit him across the face, open-handed, hard. My fingers tightened into fists. I was right underneath him, vibrating. One jab and I could have shattered his nose.

"Don't you ever swear at me, you bastard," I roared into the boy's frightened face. And even as I spoke, a small part of me noted the irony in that command.

Dick cringed and shrunk down and as he did, I returned to myself, aware of the kitchen again, of the line of boys standing ten feet to my right, eyes wide like they were watching a horror movie. I dropped my hands and Dick edged past me. The other boys moved as well. The refrigerator door opened. A soda fizzed. Key chains rattled.

I felt clammy, shaky, miniaturized. My blouse stuck to my chest. I needed to be alone, but when I turned toward the office, Barry and Mark were waiting. Barry looked at me sideways with something like pride. Mark patted my shoulder.

"The Great Nina," he said in his sweet, high voice. I couldn't tell whether he was trying to comfort me or praise me or both, but I didn't want to talk.

"Excuse me," I said, moving past them, then shutting the door.

I sat at the tiny cluttered desk. My cigar had gone out but the sour smell lingered. I put the ashtray on the floor, making room to rest my head on my arms.

In another circumstance, I might have felt proud to have been that fast and effective, but not now. This hadn't been anything I'd chosen. It didn't even feel like me. I'd never been so out of control in my life.

I was useless to the boys now. It was time to leave. They needed adults to be rock steady and if I couldn't manage my own behavior, there wasn't anything I could do for them. More than that, they were adolescents. They'd keep pushing to see where I'd draw the line. Now that I'd revealed how easily I could be provoked with just one word, someone was bound to press that buzzer again. The next time one of them called me a bitch, I wasn't sure what I'd do.

# 25

I spent more time than ever at the dojo after I'd resigned from the group home. I missed the shoving, noisy camaraderie of the boys but the karate school gave me some of that. It was also a place where I was responsible only for myself. I could walk in, change into my *gi*, bow onto the mat, stretch, then go through a half hour of *katas* without having to say much to anyone.

One Friday night, about a month after leaving the group home, Lee and I paired up to practice. It was seven o'clock. The karate school was quiet all around us.

We stood side by side, three feet apart on the worn green vinyl mat, before turning to face each other. In an instant, Lee charged at me. I slammed my forearm across his, knocking his lunge punch off target before it could shatter my sternum, and shot a roundhouse kick to his temple. He spun underneath my leg, pivoting on the balls of his feet and firing a back-fist to my jaw. I leaped off the line of attack, whipping out a side thrust kick that he dodged before it landed. Lee advanced toward me but I didn't retreat, pivoting so we faced each other head-on. Then we both stopped, drew our feet together in unison, and bowed.

"You want to go through the two-man set again?" he asked.

"Yeah. Let's switch sides. Just give me a minute."

Some damp strands of hair had twisted free. I pulled them back off my face and re-cinched my braid.

Twenty minutes later, after we'd completed a few more rounds of this brown-belt set and we'd each gone back to working out on our own, I bowed off the mat, tired, hungry, ready to leave. But I stopped on my way toward the changing room. I hadn't shopped for food. There was nothing, no one, waiting for me in my apartment.

"Feel like grabbing a bite?" I said to Lee.

He was throwing jabs at the heavy bag. He'd taken off his *gi* top and his black T-shirt was soaked with sweat. He stopped punching and looked at me, cocked his head to one side and narrowed his eyes. All we'd ever done together was train. A few seconds went by before he replied.

"Sure. Why not? I don't have any pressing engagements." He made a fake little laugh.

This was the same self-deprecating line he'd used sometimes when I'd asked if he had time to train. He didn't have a real job, scraping together just enough to pay his rent by teaching karate classes to beginning students. He was almost always free.

I was surprised he'd hesitated. Lee often trailed after me, revealing the same kind of longing I'd seen in some of the boys at the group home. I'd assumed Lee wanted to be closer to me, that he was mine for the asking.

The Pit Stop was almost empty this early on a Friday night. I led Lee toward the back, away from the bar and the long row of stools. Even without patrons, the smell of beer and tobacco permeated the air. We sat down at one of the little tables and I glanced around for the cocktail waitress. A song was playing on the jukebox that I didn't recognize but Lee did, tapping the scarred tabletop with his fingertips and slapping out the beat with his palms. I watched him for a while before speaking.

"You're good," I said.

"Nah, not now. Used to be a long time ago. I played drums in high school." He continued tapping as he spoke.

"No kidding? Why did you stop?"

"Amphetamines. Speed. I started shooting up. Rock and

roll is full of drugs. I had to get away. I've been clean for seven years."

If I'd had to pick a drug, it would have been speed. I snorted some with Paul once. The jolt of energy, the agility of my mind, the sense that I could rocket through space was exhilarating. I didn't need to hear lectures about how addictive speed was. After sampling its strength, I could imagine being seduced and didn't allow myself to touch it again.

Lee's burger came with everything. He bit into it with his eyes closed. *A musician and a drummer. A drummer and a former junkie.* I would never have guessed. Drums had to be the sexiest instrument around—the rhythm, the pounding, the endurance.

I walked over to the jukebox, slid two quarters into the slot and picked three songs. My favorite, *Heart of Gold*, played first.

"Want to dance?" I asked Lee, standing a few feet from him on the scuffed floor, holding out my hands and swaying.

He stared at me and his forehead creased.

"Don't worry. It's a slow dance. Nothing to it," I said as Neil Young sang, "I've been a miner for a heart of gold."

Lee rose, his mouth pinched tight and, looking down, joined me.

I usually came up to men's armpits, a few times I've been pinned at a waist, but I'd never danced with someone just a little taller than me before. We wrapped our arms around each other and our bodies cinched together. We barely moved.

Back in college, over games of gin rummy, the girls in my dorm debated predictive factors. Some felt it was the nose. Others favored the feet. I leaned toward hands. But none of us doubted the premise that there had to be some anatomical clue to the size of a guy's penis.

Everything about Lee's physique seemed small and proportioned, everything except the hard-on that pressed against me. A sweet buzzing vibration started deep inside me.

I tried to dampen it down. *This was my friend, my training partner,* I told myself. *This was a short man who'd dropped out of high school and didn't have a real job. I've got to stop this.* How? Humor. The best way to defuse anything was by laughing about it together.

When the song was over and we'd stepped apart, I smiled.

"Do you always get an erection when you dance with a woman?"

He glared past me toward the nicked oak door to the men's room. Even in that dim light, I could see him blush.

"No. I'm sorry. It's not something you control."

I felt awkward. I hadn't meant to offend him.

"It's nothing. It's kind of sweet, flattering," I said, glancing down.

"Yeah, right."

The drive back to the dojo in my van only took ten minutes but it felt much longer. Both of us were silent. I pulled up behind Lee's banged-up old Dodge, the only car in the parking lot outside the dark school. Lee had my car door open before I'd fully braked.

The next time I saw Lee was Tuesday, teaching an evening white-belt class. He nodded in acknowledgment when I waved as I passed, then continued calling out commands: front snap kick, upper block. I was hoping he'd see my "I'm sorry" smile, but he gave no indication if he had. Later, during the advanced class, when it was time to pair up, I darted over to him, tapped him on the shoulder and pointed back and forth from him to me. Lee never spoke much. Sign language seemed the safest way to get us back on track. He gave a small shrug with his shoulders and took the spot across from me.

By the end of class, I knew I had my training partner back. This was what I wanted. I could always find someone to sleep with. It wasn't worth risking what we had for sex. The dance in the bar was an anomaly, something Lee wanted to forget as much as I did.

After class, a few nights later, when I was sitting on the mat doing some final stretches before heading out, I glanced over and noticed Lee. He was about ten feet away, his back toward me, throwing a front kick in slow motion. When he reached full extension, he held his leg out rigidly for almost a minute, balancing on the other foot. This was an exercise we all did—nothing unusual here. But without thinking, I leaned back on my elbows and stared at the curve of his butt.

A few minutes later, when I was packing up my gear and Lee was toweling off nearby, I said in a forced jaunty tone, "Hey, you feel like getting together on Saturday night, maybe have dinner?"

*What was I doing?*

Lee didn't reply. His gaze darted around.

I couldn't let go. It was only a dinner invitation, after all.

"What do you say?"

His lips tightened.

"Yeah, sure. Why not?" he said finally.

I saw him only briefly on Friday. He was concentrating on showing twin red-haired boys a new move and didn't look up when I passed them.

By Saturday afternoon, I was like a foot that couldn't stop tapping. I hadn't formulated any plan. I just knew I wanted to dance with him. I imagined the two of us intertwined, swaying to a slow tune, almost ablaze with heat. I wanted to press up against him and feel his desire again. But where? It needed to be someplace where dancing took center-stage, not squeezed in the back by the bathrooms. I could only think of one club like that nearby, a gay bar called Pat's Place.

About three years earlier I'd gone there with friends from the women's movement, other straight women like me. We claimed we enjoyed hanging out in a club where men didn't hassle us, but that wasn't the only attraction. It gave us a safe buzz. We danced with each other and the occasional lesbian, then went home to our heterosexual lives. Once a short-haired woman with black horn-rimmed glasses worked her thigh against my crotch the whole time we slow danced. I was living with Paul then and our lovemaking was down to seven efficient minutes—including undressing, foreplay, fellatio, intercourse and afterglow—seven minutes in which I never felt as aroused as I did during that dance.

But it wasn't just the woman's sly moves that were so exciting. The smoky air and blue lighting, the sound of pool balls dropping into pockets, the piercing sweetness of a gay man's cologne—it was the forbidden underside of sex, deliciously erotic.

At seven-thirty, the time we'd agreed on, I pulled my Ford van in front of the karate school. The school was closed. No one was there.

I parked in the small lot and waited. Fifteen minutes later I started driving in circles around Fourth Street. Lee's car barely ran; maybe he'd had mechanical troubles. At eight, I pulled into Colonel Sanders and ate chicken legs out of a cardboard bucket in my front seat. Grease seeped through the container and painted a dark circle on my good jeans. I decided to make one more pass at the karate school before heading back. I didn't know what was going on. Lee was often late but this was ridiculous. I wasn't sure whether I felt angry or relieved.

It was eight-thirty and Lee was standing out front.

"I didn't think you'd show up. I wasn't sure I should even

bother coming," he said, his mouth tight, as he stood a few feet from my car.

"What are you so angry about? I didn't keep you waiting."

"Yeah, well. I'm sorry. I got hung up." The sharpness left his voice, but he didn't step any closer.

"Okay, let's not waste the rest of the evening. I thought we might go dancing. There's a gay club twenty minutes from here. All kinds of people go there, men, women, bisexuals. I haven't been there in quite a while but it was a fun place."

He pursed his lips together and frowned, glaring out at the street.

*What was making him so testy?*

I felt a surge of frantic energy. He was slipping away.

"Maybe I'll dance with a woman," I added quickly.

"It really doesn't matter to me," he replied, rapping his knuckles against the passenger door before climbing in.

We sat at the bar and scooped broken pretzels out of a black plastic bowl. The house wine was sour, the music loud. There were only three couples on the floor, two pairs of men and the other, both women. When the next slow number came on and Gladys Knight sang "L.A. proved too much for the man," I looked over at Lee. *Midnight Train to Georgia* was such a great song.

"Want to dance?"

"I'll feel like an idiot," he said.

"No one will notice. Look around. No one here cares."

I climbed off my stool and led him to the dance floor. We cinched our bodies together without speaking. I was hoping Lee would get another erection and he did. I curved into him and this time signaled my interest by pressing my hips against him. When we separated, I turned to smile at him but he looked down, glowering at the floor. I didn't get it.

"Are you hungry? Want to go back to my place? We can hang out."

*He must be starving. That was what was wrong.* If I could get him out of here, over to my apartment and cook for him, he'd relax.

I'd fed Lee once before, after his first-degree brown belt test the previous year. I had a meal ready, just in case he was alone and hungry after performing before the head kenpo instructor and a roomful of students and teachers. Lee followed me home that night and sat at my kitchen table, perspiring even though the test had been over for an hour and the air was cool, ripping into one piece of paprika chicken after another. Happy.

My studio apartment had a kitchen, a bathroom and one other general-purpose room. Paul had built a loft for me, a wooden scaffold with an unfinished plywood platform that held my mattress and just enough room under the ceiling to sit up in bed. The stairs to my perch were made of two-by-fours hammered into beams at ninety degrees, straight up. Underneath the loft, I'd created a small living room with two chairs and an oak coffee table. A spider plant hung from the loft's frame.

It was the perfect arrangement for me. Everything was my size. And the few times I'd brought men over I didn't have to entertain them in my bedroom. But best of all, the loft let me live alone for the first time. Even though my front door had glass panels and a cheap lock—and it would have been easy for someone to smash the glass, reach in and turn the knob—no attacker could break in and surprise me in bed. They'd never be able to creep up while I was sleeping. It would be too hard to make it up the ladder. The whole platform would shake. I'd hear them coming. I kept my *nunchakus* beside me, just inches from my head. There wasn't room to swing the sticks with control but they'd make a good club.

After we walked into my place, Lee didn't show any interest

in moving out of the kitchen. He leaned against the refrigerator, sipping water. When he finished one glass, he poured himself another from the tap. Finally, I slid my hands on his arms, then his shoulders and tried to angle him toward my dollhouse living room.

"Come on, we'll be more comfortable in there," I said.

His muscles tensed up and he twisted himself away.

"What are you doing?" he said.

"Isn't it obvious? I want to make love. Couldn't you tell from our dancing? From this date?"

"How do I know what you're up to? You talk about wanting to dance with women. It seems like you're just playing with me, jerking me around." His tone was hard. He glared at me.

"Don't you want to?" I asked quietly.

His features softened. I held out my hand and he took it. We kissed in the hallway and piled all our clothes on the rocking chair under the platform.

I ascended first but Lee was right behind. He had no trouble climbing the stairs. His body was carved and precise, each muscle expressed, like an anatomy chart. Later, I noticed his short bowed legs, but up there, in my loft, I saw only his perfect torso.

"What's this?" he asked after we'd stretched out on my mattress. He traced seven long inches on the back of my thigh with his fingertips.

The sides of my neck clamped down. I dreaded this moment—the same question that assaulted me the first time a lover peeled down the sheet, or a new masseuse rubbed on the oil. *What's this? What's this knotted rope branded on your leg? Entertain me with your story.*

"It's from an old cut. A man attacked me when I was a teenager."

My voice sounded like a machine that had lost its power, the last piston grinding down. *There. I'd given the explanation I always did. Now it was behind me.*

He didn't speak for several seconds.

"My father came at me with a knife when I was a teenager," he said finally.

"Did he cut you?"

"No. I was too fast for the old fucker. I hid under the table. When he'd found me, I ran. He just kept chasing after me, though, all through our house."

"Why?"

"I don't know. Drunk. Mean. He kept screaming he'd find me and kill me."

Lee was lying on his side, his head propped on his hand. He'd been attacked, too. I'd never realized we were so much alike. I ran my hand along the grooves in his bicep. He rolled onto his back and shut his eyes. I stroked his stomach. The ends of his mouth turned up into a smile. His breath changed, coming out in puffs.

In school, I sat in the first row, put my hand up first, wanted to be the one with the answers. In bed, I wanted to display the most acrobatic moves, demonstrate the greatest flexibility. It barely mattered who was in bed with me—I approached lovemaking like an actor desperate for the part.

I climbed on top of Lee, my elbows partially locked, as though I was halfway through a push-up, clinching my stomach muscles and thrusting my hips against his.

"Relax," he whispered after a few minutes. He touched my cheek with the tips of his fingers. "Let me make love to you."

Then he gently eased me down and moved with such kindness, such affection, such longing and such tenderness, I wanted to weep. This was what I'd been waiting for all along, someone to stand in the road and stop me.

Later, we lay side by side on the damp sheets. I talked about the new form I was learning, a new bumper for my car. No real content. I was making chirping sounds because I was so happy.

Lee sat up and leaned toward me. I thought he was going to reach over to wipe a strand of hair from my face. Then, without a word, he started to choke me. Not hard. Not long. But he took both hands, locked them around my throat and pressed down. He did it like he was sleepwalking—like he was in a training film giving a demonstration of strangulation techniques. Then he let go and lay back down, stiff by my side. Nothing was said. It was over in seconds. I had no time to react.

*What was that?*

My thinking came in clicks, like a shutter lurching open and closed over a camera lens. I grabbed my thoughts and tried to stop them.

*That wasn't real. It couldn't have happened.*

*It did,* I whispered to myself. *He just choked you.*

*No, it wasn't possible.* He'd been so tender. *It made no sense. It never happened.*

The next afternoon we sat in my living room underneath the loft, talking about all kinds of things: iron-hand training, changes in the Bay Area. (He had grown up in a town an hour north of San Francisco, once renowned for its chicken farms but now all suburbs.) Lee said he was always flunking classes. He'd never finished high school. He despised it. I was quick to add I'd loathed it, too, which was true, although I didn't mention I'd been voted "Senior Class Intellect" and graduated near the top of my class. It turned out we'd both been truants. So what if he'd been a stoner and I'd cut class to go to Manhattan to see the unicorn tapestries at the Cloisters Museum. We'd both signed up for sports after class and we'd both won letters. We had a lot in common. That was what mattered.

"The coaches hated me, though," he said, pushing himself back and forth rapidly in my rocker.

"Why?"

"The track coach knew I'd done drugs but he let me run because I was fast. I got kicked off the wrestling team." He stopped gliding and looked at me. "I dislocated another kid's shoulder. I didn't mean to. The guy was a lot bigger than me."

"That doesn't sound like it was your fault." I leaned forward on the loveseat.

"The coach was looking for an excuse. He didn't want me on the team. I was a street fighter, not like his pedigree boys." His tone was a combination of defiance and pride.

I could imagine him grappling with a larger boy, seeing an opening and surging in. It was a quality I admired in him, something I identified with, like the day he knocked the glasses off the smug spectator. Short people needed to be tough.

He rose and paced a few steps.

"I did the same thing one other time. To Wendy, my ex-wife. I introduced you once at the dojo. Remember?" He reached up and swatted one of the shoots dangling off my spider plant.

Yes, I recalled meeting her. She was a beautiful woman with dark hair and pale skin. But what I remembered most was her uncertainty, the lost expression on a pretty face that reminded me of Stephen's old girlfriend, Bonnie.

"We were standing in the hallway after class, arguing about something, I don't remember what. I got so mad, I punched a locker." His voice picked up speed. "She wouldn't let it go. I lost it. I knocked her down. I didn't mean to dislocate her shoulder."

"Was she okay?" Anxiety crept into my tone. I stared at him

but he was focused on the underside of my loft.

"Yeah, she was fine."

His mouth set into a hard line and his eyelids narrowed for a second. Then he let out a deep breath, leaned from side to side stretching, and without looking at me, strolled into the kitchen.

A jolt of kinetic energy went through me, the same churning sensation I felt in my gut when we lined up for sparring in karate class. On some level, I knew Lee had shown me and now he was telling me. It didn't matter how passive he seemed, he'd only be pushed so far.

*Fine. He has backbone. But he isn't a threat to me. I can take care of myself. Besides, I've known him for years. He isn't violent.*

But I was kidding myself. It was this edge that drew me in.

# 26

Lee had an on-again, off-again relationship with a purple belt at the Santa Rosa karate school. Irene was thin, about my height, with dull blond hair and the exhausted look of someone who waited tables, though I think she worked in an office. Once Lee and I started sleeping together, he never mentioned her and I assumed he'd broken it off.

At the end of our first month together, I planned a weekend getaway for us at Yosemite, the most famous in a string of parks in the Sierra Nevada mountains, a five-hour drive from the coast. It was early summer and the rivers were still swollen with melted snow. On Saturday, our first morning there, we hiked up to the top of Yosemite Falls. At the summit, we scrambled onto a boulder. I looked at the granite cliffs around us, a landscape I'd only seen in Ansel Adam's iconic black-and-white photographs. Lee sat at a forty-five-degree angle away from me, snapping the shoots off a downed branch.

"Something I need to tell you," he said, looking out to the falls.

"What?"

I already knew what he was going to say. He was going to complain about my carping about staying on the trail. Well, I was right. There were signs posted all over about that.

"I'm going back to Irene," he said.

I couldn't parse his words. I just stared at him.

"I've already told her. I'm going back after this weekend," he said.

For a second, I imagined shoving him into the ravine. I had

to get away from him. I leaped up and started running down the path, so angry it felt like sparks were shooting off me. But after a few minutes, my ankle buckled and I barely retained my balance. The last thing I needed now was an injury. I slowed to a walk as Lee came up beside me and matched my pace.

I forced myself to speak. "You've known this for a while, haven't you?"

"Yes."

I stopped and stared at him. "Why didn't you tell me before we came?"

"I wanted one more weekend with you."

He looked down and tapped a rock with the tip of his boot.

An older slender couple, swinging walking sticks, edged past us. The man said something in German and the woman glanced back. I glared at them. What were they staring at?

"If you want to be with me, why are you going back to her?" A pleading tone I didn't like had slipped into my voice.

Lee scanned my face.

"She'll stay with me. You won't."

I don't know what I expected him to say but that wasn't it.

*He's right. I'll leave him. No, this is bullshit. He's using me.*

I turned to descend but he stepped in front of me.

"You know I care about you. It's not that," he said. He hesitantly, lightly, touched my shoulder. "We're already here. Why don't we stay?"

A voice inside me said, *I've paid for the cabin. It's a long drive back.* Then, *Screw him. He set me up.* Finally, it whispered, *I can win him back.*

"I'll stay on one condition," I said, standing straighter. "I don't want to hear about your plans. I don't want to hear her name. Not once. Can you do that?"

He nodded.

The cabin we'd rented was musky smelling, the floor boards uneven. The bed was a folding cot, like something left over from World War II. The sheets were worn and scratchy. When the wall unit finally cranked on, it emitted little heat. None of it mattered. We grabbed each other's hair, ran our nails into backs and legs, had savage sex. At one point, Lee lay over me, his beard damp with sweat, and said, "I wish Irene could see how we make love. So she'd know how to do it."

Anger surged through me but it didn't last.

*I was the better lover. He was already missing me.*

The road descending six thousand feet from Yosemite was long, windy and slow. There was no alternative route and no way to make it go faster. A funereal haze had clung to us all morning, and even though we'd taken a short hike, we'd barely spoken. Just before we headed out, I'd caught him glancing at me as I packed my boots. He'd been sitting on the edge of the bed with a gaze so full of longing, I was sure he'd say he'd changed his mind. But when I looked directly at him, he stared at the floor.

I stopped to buy gas at a small town outside the foothills. The sky had clouded over. Yellow plastic flags attached to the overhang snapped in the wind. Before climbing out, I turned toward Lee.

"How much money do you have?" I asked in the same strained tone we'd been using all day.

Lee reached into his pocket and pulled out a handful of coins, adding "I've got another eight dollars in my wallet."

I had ten. My gas gauge was almost on empty. I'd need to fill up one more time after this. Between us, we'd have just enough to make it back to San Rafael. I opened my door and climbed down. Lee stepped out on his side.

"I'm going to the restroom. I'll be right back," he said, before darting around the far side of the cinder-block building and disappearing.

I slid the nozzle into my tank. The pump made a grinding sound. Given how slowly the numbers on the meter moved, this was going to take all day. Finally the handle jerked in my palm. I locked it back in its cradle and looked around. *What was taking Lee so long?*

After paying for the gas, I climbed back into the van and cruised around the building. There he was, talking on a pay phone facing a weed-filled lot. He was hunched over the handset, his back to me. There wasn't any booth, just a black phone bolted to an aluminum stand.

*He's talking to her. He didn't even wait until he got back to call her.*

My fingers tightened on the steering wheel and I drove at a slow, steady pace straight for him. It would be so easy. Just press my foot on the accelerator and I could mow him down. I was about ten feet from him when he turned, saw me and jumped back, dropping the phone. His face turned white, his hands flew up near his chest in the classic *stop* gesture. For a second, his fear delighted me. But I wasn't going to hit him. It wasn't worth it. *Just drive away*, I told myself. *Leave him stranded.* I suddenly realized how perfect that would be. Since he was so eager to be with Irene, she could come and pick him up.

I swerved out toward the street. In my rearview mirror, I saw him watching me, the phone still hanging from the end of the cord, his arms dangling from his sides.

I crept along Route 120, stuck behind a trailer truck. The entrance to the freeway wasn't for nine more miles. Until then, there was nothing but fumes. At every turn I could feel my engine burning up gas. With just two dollars left, I'd never make it home. I imagined being stuck somewhere near

Martinez, pacing alongside my van on the shoulder of the freeway while cars roared by in the dark.

*What were my choices?* The muscles in my neck locked up at the thought of going back for Lee. I wanted to hit something, but at the next pullout I turned around.

When I stopped in front of the gas station, Lee was standing by the curb. He climbed into the passenger seat and I steered my van into the traffic. Neither of us spoke for minutes.

"What would you have done if I hadn't come back?" I said finally. My jaw was clenched so tight it was hard to speak.

Lee glanced over at me, then looked out the passenger window. "I'd have called Irene to come get me. What else could I do?"

I stared back at the road. "Did you?"

"No."

Moments went by and my jaw throbbed.

Finally I turned and glared at him. "Why not?"

"I knew you'd be back."

"You knew it!"

Lee shifted in his seat. "I thought you'd come back. It's not like you to do something like that."

The wistfulness in his tone caught me off-guard. Then I realized he was playing me.

It was seven o'clock, dusk, but it felt like midnight. Outside the windshield, everything blurred: almond orchards, trailer parks, feed stores. It was as if I were driving through a dust storm.

Suddenly, right before me, inches from the van, a big dog, a Great Dane or a borzoi, appeared. It looked ethereal, two-dimensional, pale and white in the headlights. The animal was in front of me so fast, it might have materialized from air. There was no time to react. The van drove into the dog and knocked it down. I heard a muffled thump, then just the chugging of the engine.

*What have I done? Did I imagine there was an animal? Maybe the dog wasn't badly hurt? Maybe it got away.*

I didn't believe any of that.

I wanted to let go of the steering wheel and grab Lee by the shirt, shake him and scream, "You see what happened. See what you made me do!"

But I didn't. I didn't even stop. I couldn't deal with anything else. I had to get home, to get away from him, to lock the door of my apartment behind me and crumble.

We were silent for the rest of the trip. My breath came in short spikes and he clung to his knapsack, his head bowed over it, cradling it to his chest. I watched the asphalt of the freeway and the black needle of my gas gauge. By the time I crossed the Richmond Bridge I realized I wasn't going to have to stop and fill up again. I could have left Lee out on the concrete in the cold. All this had been for nothing.

At ten o'clock, I pulled into the dojo parking lot where he'd left his car, barely waiting till he'd climbed out before shoving the hand-shift into gear and pulling away.

Usually, I skipped going to the dojo on Mondays, but on this Monday, the day after returning from Yosemite, I stood in my kitchen and felt a downward pull. If I stayed away now, it would be easy to make excuses on any given night why I didn't need to go, why I could work out at home, why I'd rather hang around my apartment at dinner time and eat.

I opened a cabinet and shoved a box of granola out of the way to see what was hiding behind it. *Lee would be there tonight.* He was at my karate school every day now, teaching a private lesson or running a colored-belt class. I found an opened pack of spaghetti and pulled it down. A few hard yellow strands slid out and skidded on the linoleum floor. There was no way to avoid him unless I checked the parking lot for his car and crept in when he wasn't there. I filled a pot with water and thrust it on the stove. I wasn't going to stop training because of him. I rotated the knob to high and, for a few seconds, watched the blue flames circle the bottom of the pan. Then I grabbed the handle and shut off the burner. *Screw him. Let him slink back to the Santa Rosa dojo where he belonged. The San Rafael school was mine.*

My teacher, Stan, was emerging from the small front office, re-cinching his frayed black belt as I jerked the front door open and entered. His usual hoping-to-please smile disappeared when he saw me. I shot him a quick wave but he just stared. I passed the senior teacher, Cody, who tilted his head quizzically as I edged past him. I was sure he knew about me and Lee. So did Stan. There weren't any secrets in the dojo. They could probably guess what I was angry about.

I bowed onto the main mat and jumped rope to warm up. Lee's voice rose from the next room, telling someone to cock their knee higher when they threw a side thrust kick. After ten minutes, I decided to switch to my favorite equipment, the speed bag, the kind boxers use. It was suspended from the ceiling in the back. I'd have to pass the middle room to get to it, but so what. I wasn't going to tiptoe around.

Lee had one arm overhead in an upper block, his back to the mirror, teaching a teenage boy with an orange belt when I strode by. I paused and glared at him through the open doorway, mentally daring him to look at me. Maybe he felt the challenge, because he met my eyes for a second before gazing away. In that instant, a plan took shape. I'd hang on to my anger, amplify it and use it like a bludgeon. Eventually, I'd drive Lee out of the dojo with rage.

By Wednesday, I became aware how much Stan, Cody and the other advanced guys were stepping aside when I came in, not making eye contact, almost holding their breath, hoping I wouldn't blast them with my anger. A part of me liked this power. All my life, I'd used reason to prevail but crowds had never parted for me before. I could see how some people became addicted to their fury.

By Thursday, I knew my plan would fail. It didn't matter that Lee cringed when I passed, or even that he sometimes shot pleading glances at me from twenty feet away. He wasn't going to leave the karate school no matter how miserable I made it for him. He needed the money he earned teaching. Besides, my anger was wearing me down. I felt pummeled. I'd never stayed enraged that long and it had the same effect as a virus. By the time I let go of my anger I was exhausted, relieved it was over.

Lee taught a group class on Friday afternoons. At the end of that week, when he called time to start, I lined up along the edge of the mat with twelve other students, most of them kids, signaling I was joining the class. As senior belt my spot was next to Lee and when I stepped beside him, his arms shot out a few inches from his sides. The tension in his face dissolved. For a second, I thought he was going to hug me.

In the following week, Lee and I worked out together. We didn't broach what had happened between us, but we spoke to each other carefully, as if we were bruised. Ten days after I took his class, Lee left Irene and came back to me. He kept the apartment he shared with a friend from the Santa Rosa dojo, a sweet guy who jogged with trash bags over his baggy grey sweats to try to shed extra pounds. But Lee slept with me every night. We were a couple again.

Several months later, I was in the kitchen putting dishes away after Lee had come back from a long run. I heard the water in the shower stop, then his flip-flops padding lightly on the linoleum before I saw him. He wore hiking shorts and a fitted black T-shirt. A soft look suffused his face, a relaxed expression I sometimes saw right after a long workout, when his guard was down.

I turned back to the cabinet and slid a cup on the shelf. "What do you say we go out tonight?"

I stopped and moved a few feet closer to him.

"Okay," he replied in a sleepy voice.

"So where do you want to go?"

"I don't know."

"What do you feel like eating?"

He shrugged.

"Come on, I'm the one who always makes the call. You pick it this time."

He scratched a little welt on his calf. "I don't know what I want."

"How about a movie after?"

"Okay."

"What do you want to see?"

"What's playing?"

"*Dog Day Afternoon* with Al Pacino. *One Flew Over the Cuckoo's Nest.*"

"I don't know."

"You're making me crazy."

The idea that came to me was sudden and unexpected. I walked into the little living room set up underneath my loft and plunked down in my upholstered armchair.

"Come here," I said, tapping my lap.

Without a word, he strolled over and perched himself on top of my thighs, facing sideways toward the kitchen. He'd never sat on my lap before.

I put one hand in the center of his back and the other under his chin.

"Where do you want to go for dinner?" I said cheerfully in my regular voice. Then I dropped my voice to a lower register and replied, "I think I'd like seafood." As I spoke, I grabbed his jaw, opening and closing his mouth.

He didn't resist. I couldn't believe he was letting me manipulate him like this, but he was. His face showed an odd mixture of emotions, a combination of agitation and delight, like a child who knows he's about to be tickled. I felt a guilty thrill at something this forbidden.

"That sounds good to me," I said in my usual range. "Where?"

"Let's go to Little Broadway. It shouldn't be crowded yet," I intoned as I moved Lee's lips.

"You feel like a movie?" I asked in my own voice.

"You bet. How about *Young Frankenstein*? I'm up for a good comedy," I replied in basso.

"Great. It's settled," I said.

I dropped my hands and jiggled my legs to signal him to get off of me.

Lee rose. I stood. Neither of us looked at the other. Then we went out to the restaurant and the movie I'd picked. We never said a word about our performance that night or the other three or four other times we repeated it. But there was something immensely satisfying about it, and from the shy flicker of a smile on Lee's face afterward, I suspect there was for him, too—as though we'd just engaged in some kinky sex that was so revealing about our deepest natures it was best left in the dark.

In the fall, I re-enrolled in my old college, taking a full load of undergraduate courses, even though I already had my B.A. degree. I wanted a master's degree in social work to become a therapist, but I needed to improve my grade-point average before applying. Lee decided to become a hairdresser. He found a beauty college run by a man who'd built his reputation fifteen years earlier by backcombing women's hair until it stood straight out from their heads, then sculpting vegetable and fruit shapes with their hair. I didn't tell Lee how strange his vocational choice seemed—a street fighter fussing with curlers. I was just happy he'd found something he liked and would be able to earn a living. In the evening, we trained in karate. I was working toward my black belt and Lee, who already had his black belt by then, continued to teach.

I was accepted by my first choice, a graduate school in San Diego. The next summer, when it was time for me to head south, I told Lee it made sense for me to get settled there first. He never questioned me, but I assumed he knew I was leaving him. I was about to start a new phase of my life. It was hard to see how he would fit in. He hated getting together with people and actually talking to them. The only thing Lee loved was training. But once in San Diego, I was lonelier than I'd expected. After a month, knowing it was a mistake and that I'd be okay if I could hold out a little longer, I called Lee and invited him to move in with me. He asked if I was sure about what I wanted. I lied and said I was. So he joined me.

We might have continued living together just as we were, but two years later everything changed with a phone call.

# 27

My father's voice on the other end of the line was friendly and warm, no different from the way he usually sounded. I could imagine him leaning back in his La-Z-Boy recliner, a library book by Herman Wouk or James Michener on the lamp-stand beside him.

"Can you believe it?" he said. "I smoked for forty years, ate what I wanted for fifty. Now, after I lose weight to be handsome for Marilyn and give up smoking, I get sick like this!"

He chuckled, then coughed, the same three-pack-a-day cough I recognized from childhood. It was the sound I'd hear as he came up the walkway after work, sending me and our dog racing to the door to greet him, the happy proclamation he was home.

I had just seen my father two months before in June, when he'd flown to San Diego for my graduation ceremony. I'd been nervous about him meeting Lee. Another father might have been more critical of my pick in boyfriends, of Lee's profession as a hairdresser or how we were living, but my father appeared to be genuinely pleased to see me half-settled with anyone.

"He seems like a good man," was all he said later, and I'd been relieved.

It had been a wonderful visit. I drove my father along the coast. We took turns whistling show tunes and guessing what the song was. It was the first time in years I had a glimpse of the father I'd loved as a child. He hadn't changed. I had. Maybe getting older allowed me to see him for myself and not through the lens of my mother's disappointment.

Now my father's wife, Marilyn, got on the line, her tone factual but tight, saying my father had noticed a pain, a stitch really, in his side that refused to go away. She said he'd finally gone to a doctor who told them the cancer had spread through his body. It was too pervasive to operate but they were going to try some experimental treatments at one of the country's top cancer hospitals. Her oldest son was now head of psychiatry at a Brooklyn hospital and he'd gotten colleagues to pull strings to have my father admitted quickly.

After I hung up I called a friend, a physician, one of the brightest people I'd ever met. When I described the type of cancer to him and how far it had advanced, he gently informed me it was untreatable. I was going to lose my father.

None of this seemed real.

By the next day, panic had begun rising inside me. Everything was unraveling. I had to find some way to make things better, to regain control—but what? Then a plan found me. I would marry Lee. Never mind that I'd never wanted to marry him or anyone else, that I could barely sit through a wedding ceremony without fear I'd burst out laughing when the couple pledged their lifelong commitment—I'd make this work. I cobbled together a narrative: I'd just turned thirty; I'd obtained my master's degree; my career was under way; it was time to settle down. I bought my own story because I couldn't admit that I was frantically substituting one primary male relationship for another. My life now felt like a play, where a random event had set all the action in motion, and no one was in charge.

In early September, two weeks after my father's phone call, I sat across from my mother and her friend, Melanie, at a small, wobbly table near the entrance of a popular restaurant in Vancouver. I hadn't seen my mother in ten months, although we'd talked on the phone. She usually wore little makeup but now she had on bright blue eye shadow and pink lipstick, making her look tougher, looser, more like her new friend. This was the first time I'd met Melanie. She was just the kind of woman my mother liked—artsy, odd and confident. When I'd told my mother I had to talk to her, she'd suggested meeting here while she was visiting.

A few feet away from us, half a dozen people huddled just inside the entrance, waiting for their names to be called. Platters jangled, heels clicked on tile and a piercing saxophone soundtrack mingled with the surge of voices.

"You wanted to wait until you saw me in person. Okay, here we are. What's so important that you couldn't tell me over the phone? I know about your father's illness. I told you that already," my mother said, straining to be heard over the noise.

"I'm getting married," I said, sliding my chair back a few inches.

"Married?" She looked over at Melanie. "Married?" Then almost to herself she said, "Not to Lee."

"Of course to Lee." My voice rose, loud and sharp. "I've been living with him for three and a half years. Who else would I marry?"

She sank in her chair. "Well, you lived with Paul for years. You never wanted to marry him." She hesitated. "Are you pregnant? You know if you are, I always told you, I'll pay for an abortion. You never need to worry."

"Don't be ridiculous. I'm not pregnant."

My mother clasped her palms together on top of the table. Then she glanced down at her hands, as if suddenly realizing they were part of her, and yanked them into her lap.

"I guess my daughter's going to be married," she said. She

pushed herself away from the table and rose stiffly. "Excuse me, I'll be right back. I need to use the ladies' room."

My mother never said so openly, but I knew she disapproved of Lee. He had so many traits she disliked. He was short, uneducated, a beautician. For a long time afterward, I thought I'd traveled to Vancouver to zing her. I saw my announcement that afternoon as one more volley in our long-standing war. But that doesn't explain why I flew there. If all I'd wanted was to punish her, I could have obtained the same satisfaction by phone.

Looking back now, I can think of only one reason I felt compelled to make that trip. I was hoping she would stop me. I was marrying Lee to silence a dread I didn't understand. My mother was one of the few people who knew me well enough—and loved me fiercely enough—to recognize how disastrous this match would be and try to prevent it.

After my mother left, Melanie poked the ice in her empty glass, licked her fingers, then gave me a wide grin.

"This calls for a celebration. What do you and your mother drink?"

"No one really drinks in my family."

"You're no fun," she said and ordered her third vodka collins.

"What do you think of Vancouver?" she asked. "It's not Texas, where I come from, but it's nice. Now tell me again—I mean, your mother told me all about you, of course, she's so proud of you—but tell me again, what exactly do you do?"

I told her I wrote federal grant applications for a gerontology center at a university and added, "I co-produced a mini-series on aging that got an Emmy nomination." I tacked this on even though the TV show had been only a small part of my job and the award, which I hadn't won, was for the local San Diego stations, not the nationals. Mentioning the Emmys usually impressed people.

"That sounds nice," she said, sipping her drink and glancing around. "You're smart, like your mother."

Ten minutes went by. Even this talkative woman was running out of things to say. Smells of wine and roasted garlic filled the air. We smiled at each other. I stabbed at the shreds of lettuce left on my plate. Melanie shook the ice in her glass. We both gazed down the long row of harlequin black-and-white marble tiles, down to where I assumed the bathrooms were. Finally my mother emerged.

"Didn't either of you notice I'd been gone a long time?" My mother yanked her chair out and sat down before Melanie or I could respond. "I passed out. I was lying on the filthy floor of the bathroom and I suddenly opened my eyes. There was a Chinese woman standing over me. She kept asking me if anyone knew me in the restaurant."

My mother's face was flushed.

"The Chinese woman kept saying, 'Do you know anyone here? Is there someone we should get for you?' Isn't that odd? I've never passed out in my life."

"Probably something you ate didn't agree with you. You want a drink? Some whiskey will help settle you down," Melanie suggested.

My mother asked for black tea. She was still breathing fast but her complexion had returned to normal.

"Are you all right now?" I asked.

I felt guilty but gleeful, like a five-year-old, proud that I could have such a powerful effect on my mother.

She nodded and made a gesture like she was shooing away a gnat.

"Well, I've been thinking about it," Melanie said. "I know a terrific shop for a wedding dress. I love to shop for bridal gowns. Wore one at each of my weddings."

A week after my father's call, when I told Lee we should get married, he hesitated, but he couldn't think of a reason why we shouldn't. Even though my father's illness was never mentioned in my list of compelling reasons for marriage, there had never been a question about the date. My father was going into the hospital for experimental cancer treatments in November. The ceremony had to occur in October.

But a month before our wedding, when I started reviewing my plans with him, Lee said, "I don't want any of this."

He'd been sitting in my old upholstered rocker in the little house we rented off an alley. He rose, trudged into the kitchen, yanked open the refrigerator and started drinking orange juice from the container. I followed him into the room and leaned against the door jamb.

"I'm only spending five hundred dollars and it's my own money," I said, trying to keep the irritation I felt out of my tone.

"That's not what I mean." Lee stopped guzzling.

"What then?"

"Dancing, for one thing. I feel stupid dancing."

"It's a wedding. There has to be dancing." My voice spiked.

"I don't know how." He pinched his lips together.

"Okay." I held up my hands. "You don't have to dance."

"This is crazy. Who are you trying to impress?"

"No one," I said, lowering my voice to calm him.

"It's not what I would do." He glared at me.

"Well, I want a big party. I want it to be joyous."

"You want this big production, you do it. It's got nothing to do with me," he said, striding past me toward the front door and letting the screen bang on his way out.

My anger wanted to trail after him like smoke, but I wouldn't let it. *I don't need his help,* I thought, going through the same quick calculations I made whenever I wanted to do the things he didn't. *He doesn't want a celebration. Fine. I'll plan the wedding myself.*

During the next month everything came together, beginning with the perfect setting. Donna, an older single woman who worked at the university, had overheard me asking some co-workers, friends my age, if they could think of anyone with a big backyard. I hardly knew Donna, but she squeezed into the circle and volunteered her house, talking quickly, almost as if she had to sell me on the idea, describing how large and lush her backyard was and how it overlooked a wide canyon. A calligrapher had designed our invitations. The gown that Melanie and my mother had found on sale in Vancouver would be altered and shipped here in plenty of time. A photographer would do the shoot for a flat fee and give me the negatives. An Israeli folk dance teacher would bring her own tapes and teach everyone the steps as we went along. I'd bought a bolt of light blue Chinese silk, just the right amount to make a wedding canopy.

Every detail was getting checked off my long list, but the week before the ceremony, the energy that had propelled me was gone. By the morning of my wedding, it was all I could do to keep moving. I didn't care if the Taoist priest's plane from Los Angeles was delayed, if the short perm I'd gotten the week before made me look like Harpo Marx, or if Lee was silent and sullen on the drive to Donna's house.

But three hours later, as I stood under the wedding canopy in my bridal dress, all the anger and weariness disappeared.

# 28

When Lee turned toward me just before the vows were read, I felt shy, which surprised me, as though I'd become a maiden and was revealing myself to him for the first time. Then the Taoist priest, a slender Chinese man in his forties, lit eight candles. Their flames flickered in the breeze but held. He handed us copies of the handmade booklet we'd read and agreed to a few weeks earlier, The Taoist Sanctuary Companionating Ceremony.

Facing Lee, the priest read, "Lee, is it your desire to put yourself in harmony with Nina?

Lee had patched together an outfit consisting of dark slacks, a dress shirt and a fitted vest. He hadn't wanted to spend money on a suit and it hadn't been worth the fight. Now, standing so straight beside me, sweet and boyish, it didn't matter what he wore. He was elegant.

Lee wiped his hand on his pant leg, then read carefully and haltingly, "I declare that it is my most earnest desire to wed myself in harmony to Nina."

The priest asked me the same question and I repeated the pledge. He looked at our family and friends assembled behind us on the lawn, reading, "You have heard it from their own lips, how these two persons desire to take an oath... "

I'd planned on concentrating on his words but they wafted past me. Arrayed in my wedding clothes, I felt as if I'd floated down from a celestial plane. My dress had two tiers of organza draped over satin, with long sheer sleeves that came to a point over my middle knuckle, a detail that evoked medieval court life. Seed pearls were sewn across the shoulders and down the chest like snowflakes. When I'd first emerged onto the patio in my wedding clothes, the guests had uttered a collective moan, as if my presence bestowed a kind of grace—and I felt it had. Ensconced in white, a long layered veil masking my face and trailing to my waist, I was no longer myself. There was no buzzing self-talk in my head, no history and no future. I'd become the archetypal bride.

The priest handed Lee a red blanket and told us to kneel. Then the rector turned to a draped card table where he'd set out the wedding props, handing me an empty glass and Lee, a beaker of water.

The priest cleared his throat and read, "Lee, serve this water so that Nina may quench the thirst of loneliness and be refreshed by the elixir of your love."

Lee's hand shook slightly as he poured but nothing spilled.

Everything was going perfectly. Donna's backyard was huge, lush and private, with tall hedges framing the sides, blocking the neighboring houses from view. Between the dense greenery and the wild ravine on the far end, we could have been out in the country. A harpist stationed near the walkway off the patio had played as guests arrived. Most importantly, all the people I'd hoped would attend had flown in: my father, my mother, my brother, even Paul, who'd come to feel like a cousin.

The rector took the glass and beaker from us, handing us each a stick of incense and a matchbook. He pantomimed striking the match and nodded. I was able to get the first to light and, holding the incense stick over it, started an ember. Next to me, Lee struck one match, then another, muttering "Come on." I turned to help him but he succeeded on the third try. The rector, who'd been arranging candles and bowls on the table, didn't seem to notice the delay.

We were on the last page of the booklet. The priest took the incense from us, and held up another bowl. He gestured for us to lean forward and hold out our hands. Then he poured some dirt on our palms, stepped back and read, "Lee and Nina, I soil your hands with this earth. Be ready, therefore, to help, instruct, encourage and applaud one another."

He nodded to Lee to start. The next passage was his but Lee didn't move. I imagined he must have been trying to figure out some way to get rid of the dirt.

"You read now," the priest said in a sharp tone.

I glanced at Lee and saw his checks turn pink. But he wiped his hands together, picked up the pamphlet and started, "I shall dis..." He stopped, pinched his lips together, swallowed, and started again, saying each word slowly. "I shall discipline myself to be a speaker of happy words..."

His face grew redder with every phrase. I'd never heard Lee read aloud before and hadn't realized how agonizing this would be for someone who'd flunked out of high school. This last page was the longest and the hardest. I willed him to get through it, wishing there were some way I could carry him over the line.

His voice was barely louder than a whisper. "...a doer of loving acts so that my beloved may grow in understanding as we discover the meanings se-cret-ed in our life together."

Lee closed his eyes and pulled in a deep breath when he finished.

The rector held out a cloth, toweled off our hands and signaled us to rise. He nodded for my closest friend, Mira, and her husband to come forward with the simple gold bands I'd found at a good price. The priest read, "Accept this ring of precious metal and place it upon the finger of your companion, whom you confess loving and promise to protect."

Finally, there was only one thing left to do. The priest handed Lee a wine goblet wrapped in a white napkin. I'd wanted some Jewish elements in the ceremony. The canopy had been one. This was the other. Lee laid the glass on the ground, lifted his knee waist-height and stomped his heel on it, shattering it in one fast, hard motion. At the sound of breaking glass, people cheered and clapped behind us. Lee and I clasped hands, and in the moment after he lifted my veil and just before we kissed, I saw an expression I recognized on his face, the same wrung-out, relieved look he had when he crossed a marathon finish line. I felt dizzy with relief, as though I'd run a race as well. We had done it. We'd made it through and gotten married on this perfect Sunday.

After the rush of good wishes from our guests, Lee pulled up a chair beside one of his aunts, a sad mound of a woman with double chins and limpid eyes. I went to the buffet, filling a plate with a Middle Eastern pastry, really layers of crust pasted together with honey, to bring over to my father. He'd always loved sweets and had kept a personal supply of Hostess cupcakes, snowballs and Twinkies in the house when I was growing up.

I was on my way to his table when Donna scurried over to me. She was a plump woman with a nervous twittering laugh.

"Don't forget to remind your guests they can't come into my house," she said with a tight smile. "I don't want anyone traipsing around on my carpet."

"I've told everyone they can only use your downstairs bathroom."

I wasn't sure if she'd heard me. She peered around the lawn, scanning the crowd, making tsking sounds and squeezing her hands together. She'd been so eager to tell people at the university where we worked that she'd volunteered her home for my wedding. But when she'd made the offer, she must not have visualized what forty people would look in her backyard.

"We'll clean up afterward. You won't even know we were here," I said quickly before turning away.

From across the lawn and seated at a table, my father looked the same. His hair was combed back with gel, the way it always had been. His eyeglasses were the same square imitation tortoiseshell. It was only when I got up close and could gauge his height in proportion to his wife's that his loss of stature was evident. I hadn't realized how much cancer could devour someone in four months.

My father and his wife were sitting by themselves. When Marilyn saw me approaching, she leaned over, straightened his tie and flicked some lint off of his lapel. She had a square jaw and kind eyes, the strong face of a former nurse, a woman who'd raised three boys alone. I put the desserts on the table and started to sit down but my father held up his hand, signaling me to stop, meeting my eyes with a small sweet smile.

"Wait. I just want to look at you."

He scanned my gown, my hair, my face with a gaze that whisked over me like the lightest touch.

"You are so pretty," he said.

I gave a half smile, proud he thought so.

"I'm so glad you're here," I said, pulling up a chair beside him.

"We wouldn't have missed it for the world," Marilyn said.

We were silent after that. I smoothed out the wrinkles in the tablecloth so I wouldn't have to look at my father. All my life, my arms never reached fully around his waist when I'd hugged him—there had always been so much of him. Now he was vanishing. I wanted my wedding ceremony and the celebration to be so vivid, so powerful, they would tether him to this world.

I reached over and took his hand, lukewarm and damp. He

smiled wistfully, met my eyes, wrapped his other hand on top of mine and patted it in the slow rhythm of reassurance I hadn't felt since I was a child.

Marilyn watched us and beamed.

"Your father always wanted to see you happily married. You couldn't have given him a more wonderful gift."

This was just what I'd wanted to hear.

Not long after that, I found my brother off to the side, taking pictures. He'd added a thick walrus mustache since I'd last seen him, but even at thirty-five and a dentist, he seemed like the same sarcastic boy I'd known. When I asked how he liked the ceremony, he tilted his chin toward Paul, standing near the buffet, and said: "I always thought you'd marry old Banana Nose."

A half-hour later, when most of the buffet platters were empty, the Israeli folk dance teacher—a woman in her forties with a thick black braid hanging down her embroidered peasant shirt—stood in the middle of the yard, clapped her hands and called out.

"Okay, everyone, gather around me. I'm going to teach you the steps to an easy folk dance."

She pressed a button on her tape recorder and Balkan music played. I looked around for Lee. It was the first dance at our wedding. My father was too weak to be my partner. Lee had to lead it off with me.

I found him sitting with Ted, the assistant to our current karate teacher. Ted was Chinese, with hard eyes, a long ponytail and a Fu Manchu beard. It was impossible to look at him and not think of the word *sinister*, a persona I assumed he cultivated for his kung fu mystique. A bottle with amber-colored alcohol was on the center of the table and Lee was downing a glass. I'd never seen him drink. He'd told me he'd given it up when he'd gotten free of speed. But with his sleeves rolled up, he looked more at ease than I'd seen him all day—maybe a drink was just what he needed.

Lee gave a little wave when I approached.

"Ted brought a special bottle of some really good stuff. Ouzo. He's keeping it under his table just for us," he said.

That seemed odd. But I said a terse *thank you* to Ted before I tugged Lee's hand. "Come on. You have to dance with me."

I half expected him to refuse but he grinned sleepily, rose and let me drag him away.

The steps were easy to follow. We were the head couple. The women lined up on one side, the men opposite us. Both rows skipped together, linked arms, spun around and skipped apart.

I'd never seen Lee relaxed in the midst of so many people. He was the picture of elegance, holding his back straight and his arm aloft like a flamenco dancer. This was the graceful athlete I often saw in private. I was delighted that he'd chosen to reveal this part of himself here.

Almost all our guests were dancing: Mira, my ring-bearer, gliding with her tall husband; my former sociology professor, a hefty woman in a floppy straw hat; Lee's parents, his father in a navy leisure suit; a hairdresser from Lee's salon, a ringer for Elton John in a gold shirt, unbuttoned to his waist. Everywhere I looked, people were twirling, smiling, enjoying themselves. The party was a success!

Then I spotted my mother. She was sitting off to the side with her friend Melanie from Vancouver. My mother was glancing down, scowling, dabbing a spot on her dress with a napkin. Melanie, her hair colored almost white blond, was leaning back sipping wine. I started to wave but stopped. They weren't looking my way.

A few minutes into the dance, the teacher called out to

form two lines again. She said Lee and I should sashay down and back inside the rows twice, finally stopping at the foot. Lee faced me, clasped my hands, muttered *ready* and took an exaggerated high step. I imitated his movement, then we charged down the row, gaining speed as we went. It felt wild and crazy and wonderful. At one point I let my head fall back and saw blue sky fly by, but on our final lap Lee stumbled. I couldn't tell whether his shoe got caught in the grass or his ankle caved, but whatever caused it, he jerked us forward. For a second, I imagined us tumbling headfirst to the ground, my white bridal gown mired with mud and grass stains. But we righted ourselves and sashayed to the end of the row. When we released each other and stepped apart, Lee was grinning in a ditzy way that made me wonder how many drinks Ted had poured.

The dancing went on for over an hour. The last number, an Israeli circle dance called the hora, was the easiest and, in many ways, the most fun of all. Not long after it finished, Donna marched up to me. I'd seen her only fleetingly, standing on the sidelines, peering at my guests.

"How long is this going to continue?" she asked, clutching her hands in front of her chest.

I wasn't sure. I thought there might be more music. We still had the cake cutting. All around, people looked content, clustered in small groups, chatting. I didn't want the day to end.

"I don't know," I said.

"You said three hours when I agreed to this. It's over three hours now."

"Maybe just a bit longer. Another hour or so?"

I didn't say what I was thinking. *What difference would a little more time make?* No one was hurting her yard. But I knew, from the pinched way her words came out, why she wanted me to go. She was divorced and lived alone; she was jealous. She sighed, pursed her lips, and said we could keep the party going for a little while.

Maybe my mother was waiting to catch me alone or maybe it was just bad timing, but seconds after Donna tromped off, I saw her coming straight toward me from the far side of the lawn. Earlier in the day, she'd taken me aside and relayed a conversation she'd had with my father. To her surprise, he'd thanked her for making such lovely children with him. She'd been relieved and grateful that he wasn't still angry at her for leaving him. But now, from the determined way she pulled each high-heel shoe out of the grass as it sank, I could tell she had something else on her mind.

"I'm sick of it," my mother said when she reached me. "All I've heard, all day long, is how pretty your gown is. Why is everyone talking about you?" She paused, glaring at me. "Why doesn't anyone say something about my dress?"

My mother's dress was a light orange color with ruffles and layers that made her look pudgy even though she wasn't. She had bought her dress on sale ten years earlier, and it hadn't been stylish even when it was new.

A series of thoughts zipped through my mind. *People are talking about the gown you bought me because I'm the bride. That's who they notice at a wedding.* And then, more loudly and clearly, *I can't handle another jealous woman, particularly not my mother.* I looked around for Mira. We had bonded on many things in the past two years. A cornerstone of our friendship had been the similarity of our mothers; both required massive doses of validation. My friend had promised she'd help keep mine at bay if she started to make me crazy. I didn't need to wait long. Mira must have seen my mother's approach and my pained expression.

"Hello, Mother of the Bride," Mira said, coming up from behind my mother and touching her lightly on the shoulder.

"Why, hello, Mira," my mother said, turning expectantly to my friend.

"Why don't you join me and Ward over here, Bunny? I've been wanting to ask you about your work as a guidance counselor." She pointed to her tall Kennedy-handsome husband, who waved and smiled.

My mother glowed. She whispered something to Mira.

"Yes, it's such a beautiful dress and a very unique color," Mira replied. "I've been wondering where you bought it."

Not long after that, the folk-dancing teacher tossed her notebook into her crocheted purse, tucked her portable tape recorder under her arm and padded out to her car. The harpist asked if I wanted her to play an additional session but left when I said I couldn't afford it.

My father sat at the same table where he'd been most of the day, looking wilted but content. Marilyn, at his side, waved and mouthed "Hi, dear," to me and pointed to her wristwatch. I waved back, nodding to signal I understood they'd need to leave soon to catch their plane.

At about three o'clock, Mira and I conferred, then she called out for everyone to come to the front. We were going to cut the cake. I looked for Lee and found him sitting with Ted, the kung fu teacher, who quickly slid the bottle under the table as I approached. I told Lee we had one more thing to do and gestured toward the three-tiered wedding cake. He nodded, bobbing his head up and down, then rose and teetered, almost falling backward. But he managed to stand and, weaving as he walked, accompanied me to the buffet table. I forced myself to hold down my annoyance.

The photographer squatted in front of us and said, "Okay, bride and groom, hold onto the cake knife together and both of you make the first slice."

Lee swayed like we were on the deck of a ship while I guided our hands. The shutter clicked.

"Nice," the photographer said. "Now hold that first slice on the plate between you. Look into each other's eyes. Big smiles. Now turn toward me." Click. "Good. Now feed each other a bite of cake." Click.

Lee's pupils floated in his eyes and his lids drooped. This round of pictures would be a waste of money since he looked so drunk. Why was he doing this? I wanted to shake him and say, *Stop it. Don't disappear on me now. You're part of this.*

A few minutes later, Mira sliced the cake and passed around the pieces. I thought about bringing some over to my father and Marilyn, but when I looked toward their table, no one was there. A spike of anxiety shot through my chest. *They wouldn't have left without saying good-bye, would they?* But after scanning the faces of people on the patio, I found them on the far edge, away from everyone else, looking very different than they had earlier. My father was hunched down in a wheelchair and Marilyn stood behind him, her face pale, a black sweater masking the purple of her cocktail dress.

I walked over and knelt in front of him.

"What's with this, Dad?"

I hadn't noticed the wheelchair before. Where had Marilyn stashed it?

"I just use it when I'm tired. To conserve energy," he said in a small hoarse voice. "It's nothing."

I took his hand. His coloring was much grayer than it had been in the morning. I'd known the cross-country trip had to be long and tiring for him but I'd imagined it in an abstract way. Now the toll was revealed in his face.

"I'll see you in a month. Over Thanksgiving. When you're in the fancy hospital," I said quickly, trying to sound upbeat, casual.

"That will be nice," he murmured.

I kissed him lightly, barely touching my lips to his cheek, afraid that any pressure would hurt him. Marilyn hugged me and said again how they wouldn't have missed today for anything. I watched as she pushed him down the side path toward the curb where a taxi waited. That small journey seemed to take a long time. With each turn of the wheels of his chair, a part of me unspooled and trailed after him. When the cab pulled away, I went back to my guests, feeling exhausted and hollow.

An hour later, after almost everyone had gone, our host, Donna, poked me in the shoulder and said in a high, shrill voice, "It's time this was over."

I nodded. I was ready for it to end, too.

There was still all the cleanup to do. I knew I should change out of my wedding gown so I wouldn't soil it but I was too tired to make the effort. I walked from table to table, picking up used paper plates, while Mira followed me, holding open a black plastic trash bag. Paul announced he still had time before his flight to San Francisco, then, without being asked, began folding and stacking the rented chairs and tables. Mira's husband, Ward, piled our gifts into his arms and made trips back and forth to my car.

Only two tables had spectators at them—Lee and Ted at one, my mother and Melanie at the other.

I looked over at my mother, who was watching me with a sour expression from across the patio, and called out, "Mom, can you give me a hand?"

She clasped her hand over her heart like an actress in a silent movie. "Why should I do that? You don't invite your mother to your wedding to be a cleaning lady." She looked at Melanie who nodded vigorously in agreement.

I stopped scraping left-over food and stared at her, too weary, too angry, too stunned to reply.

Maybe Lee could pitch in and we could all get out of here. I turned toward his table as Ted emptied the last drops of ouzo into Lee's glass. Lee took a sip, opened his mouth as if he were going to speak, and vomited all over his vest. He looked down at himself, bewildered, then over at me. He stood, as if to show me what had happened, and his legs folded underneath him. He collapsed in slow motion to the grass, his body descending in stages.

"Let's get him in the house and clean him up," I yelled to Mira's husband.

Ward was big-boned and six feet, four inches. We called him forklift. He slung Lee over his shoulder as if he were a doll and hauled him head down toward the side door. Mira and I trotted behind while I called out directions, steering Ward to the only room I knew, the guest bedroom where I'd changed into my bridal gown five hours earlier. There, Mira and I stood at the foot of the bed while Ward lowered Lee down on his back.

I stared at my reeking, comatose husband, splayed out on the pink quilted satin bedspread, and pushed down my contempt. *What did I have to do for him?* He was wearing contact lenses. I needed to get them out. If he stayed unconscious for long, the hard discs might scratch his corneas.

I leaned over him, struggling to pry his left eye open. His arms, his legs, everything about him seemed rubbery except his eyelids. It was hard to believe an unconscious person could squeeze his eyes shut this tight. Meanwhile, Mira—who had found Donna's linen closet and helped herself to a stack of hand towels—was working beside me, dabbing Lee's vest.

Just as I'd wrenched the second lens out, Donna charged in. She looked down at the body, then at the bed where some vomit had rolled onto her bedspread.

"I'll have your cover dry-cleaned. Don't worry," I blurted out, following her gaze.

Donna appeared unable to speak. She stared at us, mouth open, hands up by her face like the screamer in Munch's painting. Then she started yelling, "I want you all out of here." She paced in a circle. "Now. Now. Now." She sounded like a blue jay.

When we left a little later, dusk had moved in, and Lee was still unconscious. Ward hoisted him over his shoulder again and, because my car was filled with wedding gifts, squeezed my new husband into the back seat of their Honda Civic.

I drove my car home alone, lifting the hem of my wedding gown to my lap so I could manage the pedals without getting tangled in the fabric. Our house on the alley was only eight miles from Donna's, but the ride seemed to take an hour. I had to will my car forward and I wasn't sure I had enough reserves.

# 29

On a Saturday in early November, two weeks after our wedding, we had a date for dinner at Lee's cousin's house. But at eleven-thirty that morning Lee stood in the middle of the living room, crossed his arms over his chest and said, "I don't want to go. I'll call and say we can't make it."

I closed the refrigerator door and turned to him. "We'll have a good time. Glen and Jenny are fun." Then, "Come on. This is your family."

He jabbed the toe of his Nike into the rug and stared at the indentation he'd made.

"Why are you being like this?" I said, even though I knew the reason. It was all about control.

This was the beginning of our familiar tug-of-war. On the day we'd planned to get together with other people, Lee would declare he wasn't going. I'd spend hours trying to change his mind until, worn down, I'd give up, announcing that I no longer cared what happened. At that point, Lee would relent. By the time we dragged ourselves out, I'd be weary and irritable and he'd be relaxed and smiling.

Why did I persist? Why not say: Look, we're going to perform this duet. It's completely predictable. You'll refuse. I'll wheedle. You'll pout. I'll plead. There will be tension between us all day, but in the end we'll go.

I didn't interrupt this pattern because I was too committed to the outcome. It was my job to help Lee develop social skills, even if I had to prod him. I thought about him the way legions of Victorian women viewed their spouses, the way my mother saw my father. My husband was my project, someone who, with the right guidance, could live up to his potential and become the man I wanted.

At four-thirty that afternoon, five hours after the verbal arm-wrestling began, we climbed into my car and headed out to see Lee's cousin.

Glen draped his arms over our shoulders as he stepped between us at the doorway and led us inside. I couldn't tell if he'd put on a little weight or I just hadn't noticed the slight paunch before. It really didn't matter. From his stride and his smile, this was clearly a man who was comfortable with himself.

"So how is the young married couple doing?" he asked, as he steered us into the living room. "You know, you kids better enjoy yourselves now. It only gets harder later." His laugh had a warm, rolling timbre.

Glen's wife was snatching some clothes off the back of the orange tweed couch as we came in.

"You both work. You have kids. There's no time left for fun," Glen continued, turning to his wife, smiling, "Right, old girl?"

Jenny rolled her eyes. "Nothing slows you down."

"You forgot that when I was young I was a bull."

They were both in their mid-forties. Jenny's hair was dyed the flat, even color of black shoe polish. Her chin wobbled. But she was wearing tight jeans with sequined moons over her butt, and as Glen spoke, he sauntered up to her and grabbed one cheek.

"We still have fun," he said.

She reached back, pretending to swat his hand. Some of the tension left my shoulders and I grinned at their playfulness. It felt good to be out for a change.

Later, Glen ushered Lee to their patio to start the barbeque with him. When Jenny and I emerged, carrying paper plates and hot dog buns, Lee was standing ten feet from Glen, his face set, staring at the grill. I considered walking over to him, trying to make him feel comfortable, but I decided that, for once, I didn't have to. *This was his family. If he wanted to sulk, fine.*

"Hey, here's the girls. You've got the easy job while the men are out here slaving away over hot coals," Glen said, piercing a seared hot dog with an oversized fork. Then, "Lee, why don't you set up some chairs. Take a look inside the shed."

He must have been accustomed to his younger cousin's moodiness because Glen just glanced at him with an amused expression as Lee tramped across the yard, yanked the storage shed door open and hauled out folded chairs. When the round plastic table was set, Glen skewered the wieners, piled them on a plate and waved us over to the table. Ten minutes later, when the hot dogs, potato salad and chips were almost gone, Glen said, "Everyone had enough?"

I nodded. Jenny patted her stomach. Lee looked like someone had ratcheted up the tension on the rods that held him together. He started tapping the table top and scowling at me. I knew what he was signaling. I was sure everyone did. It was clear he wanted to go but I wasn't in a hurry to get up and neither was anyone else.

Glen leaned back in his lounge chair and cupped his hands behind his head. "No one realizes how hard the CFO of a bicycle store works," he told us. "People think it's all glamour." He chuckled and I laughed along with him. Jenny reached over and patted his thigh under the table.

"Poor unappreciated thing," she said. "I have it sooooo easy at the bank."

They grinned at each other, then seemed to wait. Finally,

Glen dabbed his mouth with a paper napkin and hesitated before turning to Lee. "So what's new with you? How's the beauty business?"

"Fine," Lee said tersely, staring down at his hands.

"How's the training going, my friend? Any races coming up?"

"Not for a while," he said, shifting in his seat, still not looking at anyone.

"Uh-huh," Glen said, glancing at Jenny and raising his eyebrows in a look that seemed to say, *I'm out of cards here.* Glen paused, then turned to me with a pleasant expression. "Hey, I understand you guys meditate. Is that right? Lee was telling me something about it at your wedding."

I nodded, pleased he was interested. It was a private subject, one I wouldn't have brought up unless asked.

"So what's that like?"

"We sit in silence for thirty-five minutes in the morning before we do anything else. It's a good way to get centered, to start the day."

"A half hour! Without doing anything! I'd go crazy," Glen said, turning toward his wife and pantomiming drinking from a cup. She nodded, pushing back her chair and heading toward the house.

"Is that something you learned from the guy the Beatles went to see in India? What was his name? Maharishi something or the other?"

"I do something similar. But yeah, Lee practices transcendental meditation."

"Is that right?" Glen said, turning toward his cousin.

Lee looked up and some of the tension left his face. "It's really pretty simple. You may think it's hard but anyone could do it."

Glen proceeded to ask Lee questions about where he'd

learned it, how many people were in TM, if he ever fell asleep during meditation and what happened if a lot of people ended up with the same mantra. Lee seemed to grow more comfortable with each reply, and I was glad Glen had found a way to draw him out.

Jenny had returned with the coffeepot and Glen held his cup out for her to fill as he asked, "Okay. I get the picture. But here's the real question. Why do you do it?"

I was forming a response in my mind when Lee replied in an animated tone, "For power. In TM, you can build up special physical powers."

I'd never asked Lee why he meditated. I'd just assumed he did it for the same reason I did. On many Sunday mornings we got together with Mira and Ward to sit, and for the past three years we'd gone regularly to the San Diego Zen Center together.

Now his answer stunned me. *That couldn't be right. It was so shallow.* I began erasing his reply in my mind, seeing the substitution take place as clearly as if a school teacher had wiped the word *power* off the chalkboard and written *mindfulness* in its place.

*That was why Lee meditated. That was what he meant to say.*

When I got up and headed toward the bathroom a little later, Lee followed me.

"I want to go home," he said.

"We haven't even had dessert. Come on." I touched his forearm and felt a muscle twitch. "It's rude to leave now."

"I've had enough. You wanted to come. Okay. We're here. But I can only take so much of Glen's stories. The food is crap. Let's go."

I scanned his face. "Everyone is having a good time right now. I thought you were kind of enjoying yourself a little while ago. Can't you be a little more magnanimous?"

Lee made a snorting sound. "Can't I be a little more WHAT!"

The muscles in my chest tightened. *Wrong word.*

"Magnanimous. It means generous, giving," I said, glancing down at the orange shag carpet, then back at him.

Lee's face hardened. "I don't believe you. You just made it up! You're always trying to make me look stupid."

I muttered almost to myself, "No, I'm not."

This was the same accusation Lee leveled when I'd used *albeit* or *replete* in a sentence. All my life, I'd prided myself on my command of language. From the time I was a toddler, I remember strangers stopping on the sidewalk, turning to my mother and saying, "What a big vocabulary for such a little girl." Now I tried to scour my lexicon for anything Lee might not know. But I hated surrendering words, afraid they'd be lost forever.

We agreed we'd stay another half hour, just enough time to have the Safeway sponge cake. On the drive back we barely spoke. At one point I sighed without thinking and turned to see Lee glaring at me.

The wind had started to pick up by the time I pulled into the carport. We were the only house facing this alley and on first impression, the place had a dingy industrial feel. But the alley was almost always quiet, which was a plus, and once inside the walkway, the house itself was pleasant. It had been built on a double lot sometime in the 1940s and was separated from our landlady's home by a chain-link fence and a yard with a vegetable garden.

Lee slammed the car door and strode into the house. I wasn't ready to deal with his pissy anger.

"I'll be out in the yard," I yelled, tossing my purse on the living room floor, flipping on the outside light and walking out the door.

The garden was the best part of this house. The previous tenants had arranged the plants by color: peas and green peppers in one area, corn and yellow squash in another. All that fall, I'd been foraging here among the late bloomers, usually popping vegetables into my mouth raw. But now the stalks were brown. I squatted down in the dark by a cherry tomato plant, hoping to find one last survivor, but knowing there weren't any.

I could feel the shape of the rest of the night forming around me. Lee would sulk and slam while I'd keep probing, trying to get him to talk about the tension between us. As the evening progressed, my voice would get higher, thinner, like a singer who'd reached the limits of her range. By one in the morning, fatigue would roll over me and I'd give up and go to bed. That's when Lee would erupt, bursting into the bedroom, ripping the covers off me—his face and jaw vibrating with tension—demanding I stay awake and talk. I'd try to hold on to consciousness, lying naked and chilled despite the heat radiating from his core, but by that time I wouldn't be able to find a footing. Tomorrow, I'd say, pulling the blanket over me. No, now, he'd say, yanking it away. I'd say why not five hours ago? Why wait until the middle of the night? And his answer was always the same: because I'm ready now and I wasn't then. But I never believed that reply. If he'd been honest he would have said—because this levels the playing field—this is how I get back at you—this is the way I win.

When I came in from the garden, Lee was perched in the armchair near the door, his back stiff, staring at the center of the floor.

"You startled me," I said. I couldn't remember seeing him inert like that. I took a breath. "I'm going to make tea. Want a cup?"

He stared at me and shook his head.

In the kitchen, I filled the whistling kettle and placed it on a burner. Two Japanese masks that I'd found at a recent garage sale hung over the stove. One was the face of a chubby woman, her face rice white, her hair the same matte black as Jenny's. Her expression was so cheerful she could be a grandmother cooing at the newest baby. The other mask was a demon face, with carved eyebrows angling up over tiny eye slits, a large phallic nose and a mouth stretched into a line. Unlike the grandmother mask, this one was unpainted. The grain in the wood swirled around the contorted features, accentuating them, making them even more grotesque. I almost didn't buy this mask because it was so disturbing, but the Japanese woman selling bric-a-brac from a card table on her lawn assured me that its purpose was to keep evil spirits away.

I carried my cup out and sat on a small rocking chair at the far end of the living room, about twelve feet from Lee. His face was pinched into an expression I'd seen often lately, as though someone was squeezing his features from inside his skull. At first I thought he hadn't moved, but then I noticed he'd shifted his weight forward over the balls of his feet.

The space between us seemed to solidify. *He was waiting for me say something—but what was there that hadn't been covered already?* I could feel the muscles tighten around my eyes, the downward turn of my lips, the weight of my frustration. My vision blurred, the way it did when I focused inward. *We had to try again.* When I glanced over at Lee, he was glaring at me from across the room. I paused, leaned forward and was about to speak when he leaped from his chair and hurled his body through the space between us.

I saw him coming at me, flying through the air, his arms above his head, hands open wide, ready to grab and rip. But the jump didn't seem possible. He never touched the floor. There was no time to react. He hurled into me—a bullet, a spear—smashing me so hard he knocked me out of the chair and onto the rug. I was on my back and Lee was on top of me, his arms rigid as he shoved my shoulders down.

I looked up but there was nothing left of Lee. His pupils were huge and black. Behind them his eyes were molten. His skin was the red of explosions. Even the bones in his face had sharpened and reformed. He had become the demon.

There was a thud and then a flash of gold. My large Chinese brass vase with three-dimensional gold vines and sparrows crashed down just inches from my head. At the sound, the face over me erupted.

*He is going to kill me. He is going to grab the metal urn and smash it against my skull. Can I break the hold? No. I'm pinned.*

Suddenly, the hands let go. He released me and stood. And as he did, the blaze disappeared from his face. In an instant, I rolled to my side away from him, struggled to my feet and dashed into the bedroom. *Move. Move. Move.* I yanked some clothes from the closet and looked around.

*Where the hell was my purse?*

"I'm sorry," Lee said, trailing behind me but not getting too close. "I'm okay now. I wouldn't do anything." His voice was woozy.

*What else did I need?*

I sprinted out of the bedroom. Lee flattened himself against the open door as I rushed past. I grabbed my glasses and contact lens solution from the medicine chest.

"I'm sorry. I'm under control now," he said outside the bathroom.

*Don't turn and look back. Don't show fear. Go. Go. Go.*

I was a sprinter straining to reach the finish line. Lee followed me across the room, sluggish and slow.

*My purse?*

There it was, right by the door. I grabbed it as I ran out.

Lee stood in the walkway to the carport as I wrenched open the driver's door on my car. He held up both hands and said over and over. "Don't go. I won't hurt you."

I backed out into the alley and headed toward the freeway. I had a credit card and some money. I never had to come back.

The aging TraveLodge, under the path of jets landing at the San Diego airport and far from the row of newer motels lined up along I-8, seemed an unlikely place to search for someone, but I paid with cash and registered under a phony name just in case Lee decided to check. That night, the television news focused on the American hostages seized from the Iranian embassy. President Carter had frozen all the Iranian assets in the U.S. and the reporter showed a chart of how much money was involved. I checked my wallet again. I had forty-five dollars left. I considered calling my friend, Mira, but I was too ashamed.

The next day, I passed a newsstand out by the beach. It was November 19. In two days, my father would begin his experimental cancer treatments in a New York hospital. In four days, just before Thanksgiving, I'd be flying back there to visit him. He'd been so happy I'd gotten married. There was no way I could tell him what had happened or that I'd just left Lee. If I pretended otherwise, the lie would be obvious when he called my house. And what would I say to my mother? I'd have to admit she'd been right all along. Lee was a loser and I'd made a stupid mistake.

Shortly after the sun had set, I telephoned Lee from a phone booth. The traffic was loud and pressing against my back but the relief in Lee's voice carried over the lines. I told him I'd come back if he'd consent to two things—he'd never raise a hand to me again and he'd talk to a counselor. He eagerly agreed to both.

# 30

The fluorescent lights in the hallway leading up to my father's hospital room felt so bright they could burn through my retinas, but there weren't any smells. I remember thinking how odd that was—hospitals should reek of Lysol. I wondered if my father's wife, Marilyn, walking silently beside me, noticed it as well. Then I realized I was barely breathing.

I'd never been with anyone at the end of life and was terrified of seeing my father whittled down. But I had to come to say good-bye. And I had to be here for another reason. I'd been waiting for a decade—more—for him to say he was sorry. I knew from my conversations with his wife that this might be my last chance.

I'd reviewed my list of grievances on the plane trip from San Francisco. At the very top was his long silence after the intruder attacked me in my parents' bed. He'd never once expressed concern, not one word ever, acting as if it had never happened. And what about earlier that same summer when I'd felt suicidal or after I'd lost everything in the fire and Circe died? My father knew about all these events from my mother. *Why hadn't he ever asked? What if he didn't apologize for his failings?* I imagined bringing up one offense after another, wrenching contrition from him.

My father was sitting up in bed on top of the sheets. When we entered, he quickly straightened his gown, covered his knees and patted his hair into place.

"Look, it's my two favorite girls," he said, turning to us with a faint smile.

Marilyn stepped to his bedside, clasped his hand, kissed his cheek.

"I'm going to leave you with your little girl so you'll have some time together. I'll see you later today, dear," she said.

He nodded, watching her as she hugged me, and when she turned and paused at his doorway, giving him a little wave, my father's smile widened and he waved back.

All thoughts of confrontation dissolved and I felt a rush of relief. He hadn't changed much in the month since my wedding. He was still here. That's what mattered. I'd be in New York for three days. There would be plenty of time for difficult conversations later.

"How was your trip from California?" he said, pointing to a chair.

"Okay. How are you doing?" I said, kissing his cheek lightly, then sliding the chair close to his bedside.

He gave a forced chuckle. "They have some pretty nurses here. And the food isn't bad."

"What do they say?"

"Oh, you know how doctors are. This is an experimental drug. You never know. It just might work."

I nodded and started to chew on a fingernail but stopped myself. It was an old habit I thought I'd broken. We were both silent. He looked at the tray-table at the foot of his bed and I followed his gaze to the pitcher of orange juice.

"You want something to drink?"

When he said yes, I filled a plastic cup and handed it to him.

"How's everything going? How's Lee? How's married life?" he asked, glancing at me as he sipped through a straw.

"Fine. Great. Couldn't be better."

My voice came out unnaturally loud but he didn't seem to notice.

"That's nice."

He smiled at me again. Then he looked down and began fidgeting with his watch, now hanging loose on his wrist. As he rotated the band round and round, all the light left his features. In that silence, I studied the small man perched on the bed. My father had almost disappeared. It was as though, by force of will, he had projected his image onto someone else's frame, that he'd created this illusion for me. A rope of sadness tightened around me. For what seemed a long time, neither of us spoke. Finally he looked up, smiled, and my father's face returned to the features. He pointed to the television sitting on a shelf up high over his feet.

"Want to see what's on?"

And I did, springing up from my seat to turn the TV on, acting like there was nothing more I'd rather do than watch *The Love Boat.*

The next day my father and I played gin rummy and as usual, he won most of the games. Our visit only lasted an hour because his afternoon was filled with more tests and treatments and Marilyn would be back with him. I'd arranged to have lunch with my mother at a midtown restaurant. She was dating a new man who lived in Manhattan and was eager for me to meet Alvin.

My mother stood and waved from the back of the restaurant. I squeezed my way toward her, dodging around waiters and packed tables, past the briny smells of pickles and pastrami. She had transformed her appearance since my wedding. Her chin-length hair was permed, forming a frizz around her face. Her red lipstick was darker than any shade I'd seen her wear and she had on a new black leather jacket, emblazoned with zippered pockets and metal studs. It was an odd get-up that would have looked ridiculous on anyone else, but even at sixty-two she still seemed so youthful, she could pull it off.

The man next to her wore a Greek fisherman's cap, dark blue wool with a matching braided band, the kind of hat I associated with men who wanted to seem cool but weren't, middle-aged guys who hung around Washington Square Park checking out seventeen-year-old girls. But that impression dissipated quickly. There was something in Alvin's large brown eyes and the way he tilted back his chair that declared he didn't take himself too seriously.

My mother turned to me and asked so quickly her words almost fused, "How is your father doing?"

"They've got him on experimental drugs. But you know his personality. He's upbeat. He says that even if the treatment doesn't work, the doctors may learn something to help the next patient."

She let out a deep breath, seemingly satisfied that the news wasn't worse.

"I always said your father was a good man, cheap, but otherwise a good father and a good husband. He just wasn't right for me."

Her mouth hardened and she shot me a defiant look.

Alvin leaned forward. "Your mother told me you're visiting your father in the hospital. Yeah, well, I was never close to my father. I tried to hang out with my older brother but he didn't like a little kid trailing after him. Then he became a movie producer, a big shot, full of himself, and he didn't want anything to do with me."

The tension around my mother's lips disappeared. She turned her gaze from me to Alvin and said, "He sounds like a pompous ass, just like my older brother. He didn't want me around either."

They looked at each other and he blew her a kiss. They'd been dating—what, two weeks?—and they'd already bonded on their shared sense of rejection. Then I noticed that the black leather jacket hanging across the back of Alvin's chair had epaulets with silver snaps, identical to my mother's. Matching jackets. Incredible. They'd connected on age as well. They were both teenagers. Suddenly they seemed so cute, it was hard not to grin.

My father was dying. My marriage was exploding. Yet here was my mother, with a new boyfriend, acting sixteen. It was the kind of role reversal that used to make me crazy. Yet instead of irritation, I felt almost tender toward her.

When I entered my father's room on the last day of my visit, Ben Cartwright was lecturing Little Joe about his temper. *Bonanza* had been off the air for years but the reruns never ceased.

My father pointed to the TV, saying to turn it off. I did, kissed his cheek and settled into my usual chair.

"You know it's the oddest thing," he said. "All those years I smoked three packs a day. Ate whatever I wanted. But I give up smoking, lose weight and look what happens."

He pretended to laugh. I faked a smile. Then we were both quiet.

Today he was underneath the covers, making it easier to look at him. With just his face and arms showing, he seemed larger. He smoothed out his blanket, a thin spread the color of canned peas. I looked around the room, at the dresser with a framed photo of him and Marilyn on their wedding day, at the clock on the wall, the kind used in public schools with that jerking second hand.

*Three hours left. Plenty of time. No need to bring up uncomfortable things now.*

I shifted in my seat, trying to think of what to say.

"I'm going to see the new production of *The King and I*. The matinee performance this afternoon. I told you, didn't I?"

My father loved musicals, particularly ones with lots of pretty girls like Mitzi Gaynor or Nanette Fabray. I'd learned Rogers and Hammerstein, and Lerner and Loewe scores from him.

He nodded and half smiled.

"Remember the great shows you took me to? *Camelot*. Richard Burton. Julie Andrews. Robert Goulet. What a cast! That was the best!" My voice picked up speed with each word.

"Umm hmmm."

"Remember when you took my Brownie troop to Radio City Music Hall and we saw *Windjammer* on the wide screen and the Rockettes?"

We'd had so many good times. I'd almost forgotten. I didn't want them to slip away.

"Remember *Bye Bye Birdie*? That was a terrific show," I said.

My father nodded. "Paul Lynde. Funny guy. He's good on *Hollywood Squares*."

He leaned back against the pillows. All this talking was exhausting him.

"Want to see what's on TV?" I said and, when he agreed, rushed over to turn it on.

Long rows of bodies covered with blankets appeared. A voice said, "More teams are on their way to the jungle in Guyana to help identify the over four hundred bodies of followers of Jim Jones, who killed themselves in a mass suicide. Friends and families are still reacting with shock... "

"Not that," my father said as I jumped up to change the channel.

The hospital only picked up a few stations and I flipped through them all.

"Want to see the end of *Bonanza*?" I said.

My father nodded. I found the show's station again. Although neither of us was a Western fan, this plot seemed particularly engrossing. I scooted my chair over to get a better angle, but because the set was mounted so high it was hard to see the screen. I couldn't find a good vantage point.

"Okay if I sit here?" I asked, pointing to his bed.

He slid over and patted the mattress next to him. I climbed on, feeling the faint warmth of my father's body a foot away, and immediately regretted this move. He was bound to carry the smell of sickness, something akin to formaldehyde. But all I detected was Old Spice aftershave. It was safe to breathe. I stayed perched on his bed for ten minutes or more—it was comforting to be close to him—and only climbed down when my back hurt.

The story line rarely varied on *Bonanza*. I couldn't remember ever being surprised at the ending. On this show, the citizens of Muddy Creek, the town outside the sprawling Ponderosa spread, had turned out to be cowards. No one was willing to help Ben Cartwright guard a vicious criminal.

Ten minutes later, during a commercial for Chevrolet, I felt pressure building in my chest, squeezing the air out of my lungs so hard and so quickly I didn't have time to think. I turned toward my father and heard myself say, "I'm sorry I wasn't a better daughter."

*How could I have said that? I wasn't supposed to be the one apologizing.*

But something shifted, a cage door opened, and the words soared out like wild birds flying away.

"It's all right." He paused. "I'm sorry I wasn't a better father."

His tone was hesitant, a little sullen, as though I'd forced a confession out of him like a child.

"It's okay," I said.

We nodded at each other and a calm descended on me. All was set right. A voice in my mind poked at that sensation. *It can't be that simple,* it said, *not after so many years of disappointment.* And yet it was. I felt limp and viscous, as though some of the force that had bound me together was gone. He was sorry. I'd let go. My anger no longer tethered me to him.

Then we both turned back toward the screen and were silent. When Little Joe and Hoss finally showed up with a lawman and the episode ended, my father clicked off the sound.

# 3I

Not long after my father's death the following February, I received a letter from an insurance company I'd never heard of, telling me I'd be receiving five thousand dollars. My father had named my brother and me as beneficiaries in a small life insurance policy he'd tucked away years ago when he'd been a high school librarian. This inheritance came as a surprise, and almost as soon as I'd learned of it, I knew how the money should be spent. It was just enough for a down payment on an inexpensive house.

Later that week, when Lee and I were sitting in our living room in our rental cottage on the alley, I started selling him on how great it would be to have a house of our own. It was what our marriage, any marriage, needed. A home would make us a real couple. He stared at me for several seconds with an amazed expression, then declared he had no intention of being tied to a mortgage and even less interest in wasting his time on upkeep.

I'd counted on my persuasiveness to overcome his resistance. But when I tried again, he replied it was out of the question, too much responsibility. I sank back into my chair, pressed down by the familiar mix of anger and weariness, and said the same thing I'd said about our wedding, about dinners out, and so many things. I'd make it happen without him. I'd handle the payments myself.

Two weeks later, a middle-aged realtor built like a wrestler ushered us into his red Cadillac with fake leopard-skin seat covers and showed us five homes. The one I liked best was also the cheapest. It was a stucco Spanish-style cottage that had been built in the 1920s. It smelled of dog piss and was 850 square feet, so small it was easy to walk in the front door and out the side before realizing there were no more rooms. But it sat on a corner lot in a good neighborhood. Plus—with hardwood floors beneath the ratty gray carpet, a pair of original French doors that could be repaired, and a painted built-in sideboard that wouldn't be hard to refinish—it had potential. Even the barren rock-hard front yard, which the previous tenants had used as drain field for their washing machine, could be restored with rototilling and seeding.

We moved in at the end of March, about the same time Lee started teaching karate again, saying he wanted to see if he could get something going. He'd convinced eight of the hairdressers at his salon to enroll. Twice weekly, for an hour, he transformed an empty dance studio on the second floor of an old downtown brick building into a dojo. I'd put the word out, too, and buddies of mine from my gym had a friend, a nurse named Joyce, who wanted to learn self-defense.

By late spring Lee was training every morning. I remember one particular Friday, hearing the sound of a leather cord slapping a steady beat against our concrete driveway and pausing by the kitchen window to watch him jump rope. He seemed completely at peace, his eyes closed, his Nikes barely leaving the ground, his wrists rotating in small circles—a man with all the time in the world for fancy footwork. I stared at his routine, the intricate steps of an Irish jig, the tricky crisscrossing of the rope in front—all moves I knew well, some I'd even taught him—and felt my shoulders tighten. I wanted to be outside too, going through my *katas* in a beam of sunlight, not rushing off to work to pay for the mortgage. But the few times I'd complained about the inequality in our lives, Lee snapped that I'd brought this on myself. I had no rebuttal because it was true. I had.

I left through the front door just as Lee tossed his jump rope on our lawn, snatched up a worn blue towel and, barely glancing at me, wiped the sweat off his face. Joyce, the only one of his students who had begun private lessons, would be here soon.

Lee had moved on to throwing front thrust kicks in slow motion when I climbed into my car and shoved the stick shift into first. Before I reached the corner, Joyce's car pulled up from the opposite direction and slid in front of my house in the spot I'd just left. In my rearview mirror, I watched Lee stride over to welcome her. I couldn't see his features clearly, but I could guess what they were from the angle of his head, the slope of his shoulders. He was greeting her with the gentle smile, the soft encouraging voice he used when he taught, when the best side of him shone. My hands tightened on the steering wheel and all I could think was how much I wanted to be the one training alongside my old workout partner.

After dinner that night, when we were sitting across from each other in the living room, I let the grant proposal I was struggling to finish drop to the floor. I shifted to a sidesaddle position, dangling my legs off the chair, trying to appear relaxed. I'd been thinking about how to start this conversation all day. Except for the check Lee wrote me each month for half the groceries and utilities, we never discussed finances.

"Can we talk for a few minutes?"

Lee stopped flipping the pages of *Black Belt* magazine and looked up.

"You seem to be training more and more. I wondered how things were going at work."

"They're okay." He glanced back down.

"Are you busy there?"

"As busy as I want to be." He stared at me, then smirked. "I don't do perms anymore. I hate how fussy they are. And they stink. A lot of women want them but they're not getting them from me."

He snorted at the idea.

"Don't they pay well?"

"Yeah, but they take too long. I don't have the patience for them."

It had never occurred to me that he was turning away work. I couldn't think of a reply. I swung my legs over and sat upright, then said, in what sounded alarmingly like a child's voice, "You like cutting, though, don't you?"

"Certain cuts. I have one that's my trademark. My Princess Di cut." He slowly made a half circle in the air. "It hangs real nice."

"That's all you're doing?" My adult tone was back and I struggled to appear neutral.

"Well, you've got to specialize. You've got to do what you love." He leaned back, cupped his head with his hands and grinned.

Lee had this banter down. His choice of words, his delivery, his sneer—it all felt too polished. I wondered how often he'd recited this monologue at the salon. There was a long silence.

Finally I said in almost a whisper, "How much do you make?"

I'd asked Lee this only once, over five years ago, before we trained together regularly. He was teaching a handful of private students and the occasional white belt class at the dojo. When he told me his salary, the amount was so small I'd felt humiliated for him.

Now he hesitated.

"I take home about—what?—sixty-five dollars a week," he said. His voice carried no emotion. He could have been reading the ingredients on a cereal box.

Heat shot up to my face.

"You're kidding! That's less than I made ten years ago when

I was a receptionist."

Lee shrugged and, in a voice barbed with sarcasm, said, "I get along."

There was a long silence. Then he looked down at the magazine in his lap and acted like he was reading again.

I couldn't move. There was too much pressure in my head, as though I'd been dragged underwater and there hadn't been time to equalize my ears. *Look at the load I was carrying! Look at the price!* I wanted to shake him. I'd had no idea how much he'd freed himself or glimpsed the depth of his contempt. *How stupid I'd been to allow this. What a sucker I'd become.*

Over the course of the next week my anger subsided and an awareness set in. I had turned into my mother, the sole breadwinner, the wife who worked at a job she despised while her unemployed husband puttered around the house. Of course I'd thought of this before—often, in fact—but I'd always had a slew of reasons why it couldn't be true. Lee was nothing like my father, physically or in temperament. Now, all of my rationales fell away as though my father's death had incinerated them. It seemed obvious. A mantra took shape in my mind and I began to hear myself chant: *I can't do this anymore.*

The parking lot at Mission Bay was almost empty on a Tuesday evening in August when Lee and I pulled up at dusk. I hadn't anticipated it would be so quiet when I'd suggested coming here for a picnic. On Sunday mornings, when we'd driven to the park to join other runners and jog along the bay, we were lucky to find an open spot. Out on the field, a shirtless boy in his teens tossed a Frisbee for a golden retriever with a blue bandanna around its neck. A young woman, probably the mother, stood behind a little girl on a swing, arms out, ready to give her daughter the next boost. Not much company, but their very presence was enough to serve as my bodyguards.

In the nine months since Lee had jumped me, he'd kept his literal word and never laid his hands on me. But he'd found another way to act out his rage. A few times, when we were sitting at the kitchen table disagreeing about some small thing, he'd leap out of his seat and start hurling whatever unbreakable thing he could grab—a pot, a lid, a fork—past my head. I sat rigid in my chair while the barrage flew by, hearing everything slam into the wall behind me. Sometimes he stopped throwing things and started punching the air, still ten feet away from me. When I'd try to rise, to use that pause to escape, he'd grab another pan and shoot it past me. I'd lower myself to my seat again, waiting for this seizure to end.

Oddly, while it was happening, I wasn't frightened. I believed he'd keep his promise and never make contact again. Although I hated being pinned and would have felt deeply ashamed if anyone found out, I told myself that I could do this if that's what it took to keep us together. After all, he wasn't hurting me. It was a safe way for him to vent his anger. His rage was bound to be finite and eventually he'd use it up. This was just a phase he was going through. Besides, these episodes rarely happened.

A part of me even felt superior because I was the one who stayed calm while Lee was torqued with fury. So I sat there, motionless, the knife-thrower's wife in the circus.

But on a deeper level I knew I had to heal him before he harmed me. If I could do that, if I could wait Lee out and transform him, something titanic would happen. It would be as though I'd calmed violent men everywhere.

Now Lee looked out at the bay, then grabbed the handle on the passenger door.

"Wait!" I said, my mouth suddenly dry. "We need to talk."

He released his grip and wrapped his arms across his chest. He was wearing a fitted black T-shirt and even at rest the definition in his arms was visible.

"Yeah, what is it?" There was a flicker of irritation in his voice, like the snap of a cat's tail.

*He knows something is wrong. He must have noticed I didn't pack any food.*

I swallowed, inhaled, then said, "I can't go on like we've been. Something has got to change." I paused, reaching for the harder thing. "You've got to earn more money. I can't be the only one."

I'd been looking straight ahead, but I forced myself to glance at Lee. He stared at the grass and the hills beyond. His jaw locked down and a muscle twitched.

Somewhere behind us a car engine shut off. I heard a woman's voice giving instructions and the squeal of young children. Their voices were high and eager, but something about the sound made me think of china, of dishes about to break.

"The picnic was a lie, wasn't it?"

"Yes."

"You tricked me to get me out of the house. Were you afraid I'd attack you?" His tone was mocking but it had an edge.

"I didn't feel safe saying this to you. I thought it would be better to get out in public."

A knot the size of a walnut swelled in Lee's jaw.

On the bay, the wind lifted up tufts of water and stripped them of their color. Lee turned to stare at the whitecaps, his lips pinched so tight they disappeared.

"You need to pick up some costs. I don't want to be the only one working." The words rushed out, faster than I expected. "I don't get to choose what assignments I do at the university.

I can't tell my boss I don't feel like writing a grant. It isn't fair that you pick what kind of cuts you do. You could easily earn more if you wanted."

I looked over at him, waiting for a response, and found myself saying, "Things have to change or the marriage is over."

*Where had that come from?*

Lee radiated so much energy the car should have shook. My tone dissolved into a plea.

"I want time to train, too. I miss it so much. I need your help to do that. Do you understand?"

He kept staring at the water, sliding his jaw from side to side.

I waited. When I spoke, my voice came out low but certain. "I don't need to see much. Just a little difference to know you're trying. In one month—or it's over."

*There it was again.*

It was as if someone else were talking through me, a gambler who'd sized up the stakes and doubled down.

Time went by. So much pressure had built up in the car, it felt like the rivets could pop.

"All right," he said without looking at me.

"Really?"

"I said I would."

"I'm so glad."

It was what I'd hoped for. If he loved me, he'd change. He'd want me to be happy, too. I turned the key, started the motor and drove us home.

The next week, when I was in Los Angeles for a three-day conference, I called Lee each evening at dinnertime. He sounded confident and decisive. Work was going well and he was enjoying it. When I returned, the change in him was clear. He left for the salon earlier and came home later. I felt more optimistic than I had in a long time.

Midway through the following week, a new women's study group I'd signed on for was starting. The organizer, a friend from graduate school who was active in the Jewish community, invited me to the upcoming eight-week session at her home. We'd read and discuss selected books on the Hebrew matriarchs. It had been years since I'd been in a discussion group with other women, and I still missed it. It sounded perfect.

"Remember, I'll be back about nine-thirty or ten tonight," I said, turning to Lee as I headed out. "You have any plans?"

"Nope. None." He followed me and kissed my check before adding, "Have fun."

My friend, Sandy, greeted me at her door when I knocked, then led me to the living room where several women were arranging big throw pillows in a circle on the floor. Sandy was my height, in her late twenties, with the all-out energy of a six-year-old. Her house was filled with bright blues and greens in whirling floral designs and practical modern furniture. Photos, mostly of her and her husband as camp counselors by a lake, waving at the Western Wall, or beaming into the camera on their wedding day, seemed to be everywhere.

About ten minutes later, when everyone had assembled in the circle and introductions began, I studied the interesting faces around me. They looked like the kind of women I'd like to know. I struggled to come up with what I'd say when my turn came—maybe something about the women's studies groups I'd been in, how I knew Sandy, or my limited knowledge of Judaism. But I couldn't hold on to my thoughts. A swirling sickness, like the flu, suddenly enveloped me. By the time the fifth woman introduced herself, it felt like an electric current was coursing through me.

"I'm sorry," I said, rising. "I feel really ill. I'd better go home."

As Sandy walked me to the door, I promised to call her soon.

Forty-five minutes from the time I'd left, I pulled back into our driveway. The house was dark. I called Lee's name as I checked each room. The air inside felt dusty, distorted, like a place that had been deserted for years. When I returned to the living room, feeling the weight of the silence, I knew where he had gone.

I'd only attended a few of Lee's new karate classes, not sure, despite his invitation, that he wanted me there. The last time had been several months earlier. Partway through that session, after he'd announced that everyone would spar, he turned to me and said, "Give Joyce your protective gear. You don't need it and she does."

No one shared their personal equipment like that—besides, mine was new and expensive. But his request so surprised me, I couldn't think of a response. He followed me as I squatted down in front of my gym bag, pulled out my red forearm and shin guards, and handed them to him. He carried the pads over to Joyce. When she teetered as she tried to pull the shin guard over her foot, he signaled her to sit down and, kneeling in front of her, pulled the protective gear up over her calf. I couldn't hear what he was saying but he looked earnest, encouraging. She cocked her head toward him and nodded.

After he'd finished suiting her up, Lee waved for me to join them, said to pair up, then strode off to deal with other students.

Joyce and I bowed to each other. She was a few inches taller than me with unmemorable features and dark blond hair styled in the Princess Di cut that Lee liked to do. I stepped back into a relaxed fighting stance but she just stood there. I moved in slow motion and threw a roundhouse kick to her head, careful to stay out of range. She raised her arms to cover her face and tucked her head down. I slid closer in and lightly punched the air in front of her, then tapped her forearms to let her know she should block. Lee had been sparring half-speed with the hairdresser who looked like Elton John, but he suddenly darted over before the two-minute round was up.

"Stop it," he said to me in an angry tone. "You don't need to go at her so hard."

"I pulled everything. I was going slow." My voice had a whiny edge.

"You don't need to show off. She's just a beginner."

He patted Joyce's shoulder and said softly, "You're doing fine."

His response hadn't made sense at the time. *Maybe I was showing off a little but I hadn't touched her.* My ability used to make him proud. *Why was he carping at me?*

I turned off all the lights in the house, climbed back into my car and headed west. Joyce's address had been easy to remember because it was so distinctive: 10 Texas Street. I'd never been there, but I'd helped Lee send letters to his students telling them what to bring for the first class.

*He's there. I know it. No, that's ridiculous. I'm overreacting.*

The words formed a loop in my mind. I was almost there when another car flashed me and I realized I was driving blind. I'd been so upset, I'd forgotten to turn on my headlights.

*You'll see. He's not going to be there,* I told myself as I switched on my lights.

But of course he was, his dented green car nuzzled up to the curb in front of her house.

# 32

I wailed all the way home. When I got there I curled up in the dark on the living room floor, tears and snot streaming out of me, unable to move. Each time I tried to steady myself I couldn't stay on the surface. *It was over.* Eventually, after what seemed like a long time, another thought cut through that torrent. *How dare he!* I rose, paced the room, feeling the muscles in my arms tighten and wanting to punch something. But that anger buoyed me for only so long before the realization of what was lost dragged me back down. It went on like that for over an hour, desolate one minute, seething the next.

At nine-fifteen, a car eased into the driveway, footsteps bounced up the walk, a key felt its way into the lock, and Lee strolled through the doorway.

"Where were you?" I said as he stepped inside, my voice hoarse and raw. I was sitting at the far end of the darkened living room.

Lee stopped and hesitated for a second.

"At the gym," he said, turning on the light.

"Liar," I shouted. "I know where you were!"

I leaped out of the chair and charged at him. He hunched sideways but didn't try to block.

"Liar!" I stood a foot away, facing him dead on, and slammed him against the wall. This was a man who could have taken my head off but I knew he wouldn't. He'd be too ashamed.

"How long have you been sleeping with her?" I yelled six inches from his face.

"Two weeks."

He looked down, cringing.

"How could you do this?"

"She came on to me."

I stepped back a few feet, feeling my face harden. *What bullshit.*

"You gave me that ultimatum," he said, glancing at me before quickly looking away. "I knew I'd never meet it."

He edged past me, but stopped and turned when he was halfway across the room, anger sparking in his eyes.

"I wouldn't make money when my first wife wanted me to. I wouldn't do it for myself. I certainly wasn't going to do it for you."

I was breathing hard. I wanted to smash something.

"You were going to throw me out. Joyce is a good woman," he said in a pleading tone.

Suddenly, the shadow of a question formed in my mind. I peered around the room, at the little couch I'd just had recovered in a Japanese fabric with stylized blue outlines of cresting waves, then at the kimono embroidered with rainbow-colored flowers hanging from a pole on the wall.

"Where did you get it on with her? Here?"

He stared at the floor, silent.

"While I was at the conference in L.A.?" I said.

"Yes," he said, his voice barely audible.

"Where?"

"She came over."

There was a pause. In my mind I saw them whispering in the living room and Lee guiding her by the hand to the hall.

"In our bed!" I shouted. "You got it on with her on our sheets!"

Our bed was an extension of my body, holding my smells, my warmth. Surging behind that image came a realization. The bed was imbued with our sex, our fluids, our sweat. He'd defiled everything.

All the anger left as suddenly as a lamp turned off. I crouched down in the corner of the living room, behind the shedding ficus tree, covered my head with my arms and sobbed. I wanted to make myself so small I'd disappear.

Later, a toilet flushed, a door squeaked shut. On the other side of the wall I heard Lee's footsteps moving around the bedroom, then the mattress creak. I straightened up slowly, walked to the hall, grabbed some linens from the closet, spread them on the couch, and lay down in the dark.

The light from the street slanted in through the half-finished French doors. I could see everything—the spider plant dangling its shoots down the stand, the little rosewood Chinese table, the floor lamp with a milky glass shade. But the objects seemed as flat as images on a movie screen.

*Joyce. That mouse. Her washed-out blond hair. Always smiling, pretending to be so sweet. I should have pummeled her when I had the chance. I wasn't going to lose Lee to her.*

I threw the blanket off and strode into the bedroom, pausing a few feet from the mattress where Lee lay on his back. His features were white and wooden, his eyes open and his gaze focused on the ceiling.

I peeled off my T-shirt, my underwear and stood naked.

"What are you doing?" he whispered, turning his face toward me. The rest of his body hadn't moved.

I knelt on top of him, straddling his chest. My hands slid from his shoulders to his arms, finally down to his wrists, where I pinned him.

"Are you sure?" he said, his voice frightened and hopeful.

I lowered myself down and took him in. He had to remember who the better lover was, to long for what he'd lost.

"Do we still have a chance?" he asked, so quietly he might have been talking to himself.

I didn't answer because I didn't know. I was only certain of one thing. I had to regain control, to take back what was mine.

In the weeks that followed Lee and I continued living together—only now there were no discussions about money—instead, our tense conversations centered on whether he'd stay with me or move in with Joyce. I understood how the power had shifted between us but I felt helpless. It was just like a grappling move we'd practiced in karate. One minute I had Lee in a wristlock but seconds later he'd counter-grabbed, locked back my elbow and seized control.

The marriage counselor was in his forties with the inquisitive, slightly bored expression of a high school science teacher. His office, in a cinderblock high-rise that housed insurance companies and temp agencies, was such a no-nonsense place we could have been there for a tax audit. There was no box of Kleenex on the desktop, no soft lighting, just a six-foot potted rubber-tree plant, a crammed bookcase and a wide metal desk with his chair on one side and the two we sat in on the other.

On our first session, the counselor and I established a quick rapport while Lee sat with his arms crossed, hunkered down in his seat, glowering.

Midway through our second session, while the counselor was laying out what he called "the rules for communication in a marriage," Lee started squirming in his chair, tapping his hands on the tops of his thighs. Then, leaning forward, he blurted out, "She let one of her boyfriends tie her up." He paused and added, "She liked it."

The counselor stared at him before replying.

"So what? Don't you have sexual fantasies? Don't you ever act on them? Doesn't everyone?"

For years, I'd felt guilty about Stephen and wished I'd never told Lee about our sex life. Now, with one stroke, all that shame was wiped away. Everyone had secret desires.

The counselor turned back to me and said in a pleasant tone, "Have you talked about sharing finances before?"

I nodded. I'd come right from the university, still in a pink and brown plaid blouse, polyester slacks and cultured pearl earrings. I fidgeted with my earring, about to respond, when Lee thrust his weight hard against the back of his chair.

"I feel like jumping out the window," he shrieked.

He was wearing a green T-shirt, the shade used for camouflage, and the color made his face, which was already flushed, look crimson. The counselor didn't reply, but he glanced at Lee and shook his head.

Although I'd never heard Lee threaten to hurt himself, I recognized this fury. If we were home, he'd have punched another hole in the wall by now. But sitting here, in this air-conditioned office, all he could do was flail. Suddenly, it was as if I were witnessing this part of him, this tantrum, for the first time—as though the marriage counselor had dissected Lee's behavior and signaled me over to a microscope to study the slide.

I looked past Lee to the window. We were on the third floor. *Good,* I thought. *Jump. You'll just break your legs, jerk.*

A few nights later, close to midnight, Lee and I filed into Denny's. The restaurant had become our safe house, where we went when he started hurling lamps or putting his fist through the sheetrock. The first time I'd suggested we get out of the house to talk he'd seemed relieved.

The waitress had red hair, a blue uniform and two large plastic menus under one arm. She looked over our heads, toward us but not at us, and asked in a flat voice if we knew what we wanted. When we shook our heads she handed us each a menu, saying she'd be back. Lee and I hadn't spoken since we'd sat down. Now we stared at the photographs of glistening hamburgers and pancakes drenched with something that looked like motor oil. We ordered chef's salads. Later, after the waitress had brought us coffee, I picked up my fork and tapped the bottom on the table, prongs up.

Lee watched me with half-closed eyes.

"Put that down," he said in a low, strained tone.

"Why? You think I'd use this as a weapon?"

The idea was ridiculous.

"Just put it down," he said.

Lee had told me the story of how his drunk father had stalked him with a knife when he was a teenager. I must have heard it fifty times. How, if he hadn't hidden, his father would have stabbed him, probably killed him. The story always won my sympathy, but up until that instant I'd never realized just how frightened Lee had remained—of me, and maybe of everyone.

One night in mid-December, almost four months after my ultimatum, the air had chilled. The rainy season was starting. I turned up the heat in our house for the first time since the previous winter and dust puffed out in clouds from the floor vents. I brought two plates of black beans and brown rice to the table. Lee pulled out a chair and joined me.

We ate in silence. The only sound was the utensils scraping against the plates.

When we'd finished, I asked the same question I'd been posing for months: "What are you going to do?"

He squeezed his eyes shut, then pushed back from the table with both hands.

"I haven't made up my mind."

I studied his face.

"We don't have much time left to make it work."

I couldn't say how I knew this but I sensed a change inside myself. It didn't even feel like something I was choosing. It was more of an inexorable shift.

Lee didn't meet my eyes.

"I haven't decided yet," he said in a prissy voice.

He stood, started to walk to the bedroom but stopped, turned back toward me and added, "Everything with you is so much work."

A few minutes later, he emerged wearing his dark blue jacket, his army surplus backpack dangling from one hand. I hadn't even realized he was planning on heading out.

"Where are you going?"

He let the backpack drop to the floor and yanked up his zipper. The muscle in his jaw twitched.

"You're not planning to see Joyce, are you?"

"I'm going to the gym," he said.

"Remember what the marriage counselor said, no seeing her while we work things out."

"Yeah."

"You promised."

"I said I know. Don't push me." He slammed the door on his way out.

An hour later, at about eight, the phone rang. *It might be Mira calling to set up plans for the weekend. No, it's probably Lee. His clunker finally broke down and he needed a ride.* I picked up the phone, feeling irritated but resolved.

"Is this Nina?" the man's voice was low, jagged and unfamiliar.

"Yes, who is this?

"We've got Lee."

"Who is this?" I said.

Was this someone from Lee's hair salon playing a joke? The question barely formed before I knew it wasn't.

"Listen to me, bitch," the man said, his voice rising. "We've got him here. Tied up. You do what I say and he won't get hurt."

My thinking became murky. *How was that possible?* I couldn't imagine Lee surrendering. *How many were there?* They must have surrounded him, jumped him, clubbed him. *Was he still conscious?*

"Are you listening to me?" he said.

"Yes."

The telephone receiver grew heavy in my hand, a barbell I could barely hold.

"Then answer when I talk to you." His voice was sharp with rage.

"What do you want?"

I was aware of the skin covering my face, my lips, the cords tightening at the back of my neck.

"Shut up. I'll do the talking. You do as I say. You understand me? What are you wearing?"

I looked down at the body underneath me. It no longer felt like mine.

"A blouse. Jeans."

"Take off the blouse, bitch."

The walls, the furniture blurred. All the color left the room. I knew I was standing but there was no sensation of the floor.

There was a long pause.

"What are you doing! Did you hear me? Take off your blouse."

The voice tightened like a wire wound around my neck. My free hand started toward the top button, then froze. Suddenly, I was pinned in my parents' bed with a man hovering over me. It was as though I could observe the scene from across the room, over the inky black of the man's shoulder, except he wasn't a man—he was a hole in the universe. But I could see myself, the strands of dark hair matted to my cheek, the blue and green daisies on my sleeveless nylon gown. I heard a girl's voice say with calmness and certainty, "You don't want to do this." I saw that girl and remembered her resolve: *He'll have to kill me or knock me unconscious. I will not submit.*

I wouldn't capitulate to save myself thirteen years ago. Why should I cower for Lee now?

"No. I'm not going to do it," I said, dragging the words out, straining against the exhaustion that suddenly engulfed me.

"What?" His voice spiked up. "What are you saying, you stupid cunt!"

"I'm not taking my clothes off," I said louder, clearer.

"Do you understand me, bitch. We have Lee. If you don't do what I tell you, you'll never see him alive again. We'll kill him."

He was almost screaming. I imagined spittle forming at the sides of his mouth. Outside, the fronds of a palm tree rustled in the wind. My ribs rose and fell with my breath.

"Then you'll have to kill him," I said, and set the phone back in its cradle.

# ZEN GARDEN

# 33

If this had been a movie, the camera would have zoomed out as I hung up the phone and the credits rolled, but this was life. Within minutes, I panicked. I began a phone search for Lee, calling his gym, the Zen Center, even Joyce, and finally my friend, Mira, for comfort. At nine-fifteen, Lee strolled through the door, wet with rain and unharmed. He snapped at me when I told him I'd tried to track him down, but when I pressed, he said he'd been at the gym the whole time and was probably showering when the guy from the front desk had checked the locker room. I believed him. Some psycho must have searched for a man's and woman's name listed together in the phonebook and figured, if it were early enough in the evening, he'd catch the woman alone.

But that call woke me up. I stopped asking Lee what he wanted to do because it no longer mattered. It was over. Right after a gray New Year, I told Lee he had to move out. He wasn't surprised. He stuffed his belongings into his car and headed back to northern California.

That first month I was a mess. Mira kept me close, saying I shouldn't be alone, and I was grateful.

I was also lucky.

It was 1980. The San Diego real estate market was soaring and so was the interest rate. It seemed likely that I could sell my house for a profit because my mortgage rate was lower than the one banks were now charging, and it was the kind of mortgage that could be taken over by the new buyer. I just needed to make my house presentable.

For six weeks, my nights and weekends were devoted to restoring the French doors and sideboard, hanging wallpaper and retiling the kitchen floor, all repairs I'd imagined Lee and I would have tackled. In the spring, not long after my house went on the market, a gay couple was charmed by all the little architectural details that had originally captivated me. They agreed to give me my asking price if they could assume my mortgage and owe me the difference, paying me a fixed amount each month and settling up with one big payment in five years. This form of finance was new to me and it turned out to be ideal. Their monthly check didn't amount to much money but I could live on it for a while if I were careful. So I sold my house in Normal Heights, resigned from the university and found a small garden apartment just blocks from the bay and only a few miles from the Pacific.

I knew what I needed to do next. I had to work out a program to change. If I didn't, the next man I found would be a version of Lee and the pattern would keep repeating. I was still a wreck—Mira said I was the consistency of wet cement—but I recognized I had been given an amazing opportunity, one I wasn't about to waste. Transformation became my full-time job.

I began training on many fronts and my days became structured and full. I kept a journal and recorded my dreams as soon as I awoke, then meditated for a half hour. I reclaimed the physical realm I'd loved but had relinquished to Lee: running, weight training and yoga. I did silly, sensual things for the first time in my life, like lying out in the sun each day, tanning, to see how dark I could get. (Very.) I saw a Jungian therapist once a week. And at peer counseling sessions, where gaining personal power seemed to be the universal goal, I was the only one who longed to be rid of her hard shell.

The nights became my place for mourning. That was when the full weight of my loss and loneliness hit. During the day, I'd stopped listening to the car radio because every insipid song was suddenly infused with meaning and I found myself weeping on my way to buy groceries. But at night, I wanted to feel. I'd lower the stereo needle on the Bette Midler album with *The Rose*, lie on my living room floor, crunch myself into a ball, then rock and moan and cry while she sang, "Some say love, it is a razor that leaves your soul to bleed... I say love, it is a flower and you its only seed."

When I'd first quit working, I'd imagined an eight week hiatus before finding a new position. But six months after I'd sold my house, I was still emotionally wobbly with no desire to curtail my inner work. Usually my mortgage check generated just enough to get by, but in October, when I was still a week away from receiving those funds, I found myself almost out of food and late on my rent. I had to do something for cash fast.

# 34

Selling things at the flea market was the quickest way I knew to raise money. On Columbus Day, I packed my latest car, a used green Datsun Honeybee, with a handful of small treasures that had been in my closet for years, including a Chinese embroidery of stylized blue bats, my collection of Dr. Strange comic books and a fake gold bracelet with a charm that read "Nixon." But when I pulled into the parking lot where the swap meet was held, I was seized with the feeling that this wasn't where I was supposed to be. I was needed at the Zen Center.

Two weeks before, I'd received a flyer from the center asking for help at their fall community workday. At the time, I'd mentally signed up. It seemed like the kind of thing I should do. I'd meditated there so often, I wanted to give something back. But as the date drew closer and my bank account dwindled, I'd lost the luxury of volunteering.

Now, sitting in front of the flea market, so close to setting up my table and making some extra cash, I felt compelled to shift the car into gear and drive eight miles north to the Zen Center. When I got there, I stopped just off the road and looked up the hill. I could see the meditation center, the almost empty parking lot, but I couldn't force myself to go there. *There'd be other workdays. What I needed now was money.* I turned my car in the opposite direction and retraced my route. This was getting to be ridiculous. I'd been indecisive before but I'd never felt slammed back and forth like a tennis ball.

On the second drive to the flea market, I assured myself

that this was the right choice, but once there, I couldn't budge from the front seat. Something at the Zen Center was dragging me back, reeling me in like a physical force. I glanced at the knick-knacks crammed in the seat behind me. The flea market would be there again next week. I could make it through until then with the food I had on hand. My landlord could wait. I started the car again, made a U-turn and checked my watch. There was still time.

The Zen Center was a one-story building north of San Diego that sat by itself on a large tract of gently rising land. I parked and trudged over to the group assembling in front. There were about twenty people, most of their faces familiar, but I noticed a few I hadn't seen before. One was a slightly overweight man standing off by himself on the hillside. He had a thick mustache and bushy beard, brown with glints of red in the sunlight. His shirt was off and his face was tilted up to the sky. I looked at him, at his small paunch, and thought, *I could even date someone like him.*

A little later, a monk I'd seen a few times called everyone together. He pointed to those standing on his left and said that group would work in the house, buffing the hardwood floors, cleaning windows. The others would restore the garden. I was part of the second group. So was the man with the beard.

It was perfect weather to work outside, a classic San Diego day in the seventies, with a cloudless sky, no humidity and a cleansing breeze from the ocean. When my group fanned out, I picked up a rake and trowel. The man with the beard ambled toward the back of the garden and started working a machine that looked like a small plow. There was plenty to do. The soil in the big vegetable garden was hard-packed from months without rain or tending. Thorny weeds clustered around dried-out stalks of corn and tomatoes. I crouched down, digging at the base of the weeds, trying to expose enough root so I could yank them out.

After fifteen minutes, I strolled over to the man with the beard. He'd put on his shirt, a tan canvas fabric with rolled-up sleeves, and was pushing the machine through the soil, carving out rows of freshly turned earth. I'd been curious about these devices for a long time but had never seen one up close.

"Is that a rototiller?" I asked, pointing to it.

"Yes." He stopped and looked at me pleasantly.

"Do you mind if I try it?"

He demonstrated how to give it gas, a simple direct explanation that was easy to understand, then moved aside. I grabbed the handles and leaned my weight into it. The machine lurched and bounced on the ground, barely moving a few feet. I strained to keep it steady and cut a clean line, but it was all I could do to get forward momentum.

"Why don't you take over again?" I said, stepping away after a few minutes.

The man with the beard nodded. He must have known that I didn't have the body mass to push through the packed earth, yet he'd said nothing. I liked him immediately. If he'd told me I was too small, or worse, that a woman couldn't do it, I would have hung onto that machine, straining to keep it moving, until the sun went down. I went back to weeding and he continued to turn the soil.

We started talking a little later, ambling over to a stone wall and sitting down. His name was David. He said he was a psychology professor from upstate New York here on sabbatical and had been given an office at a nearby university. He'd grown up in Southern California and this was his first chance, after ten frozen winters, to come back to the sun. He'd been divorced for four years and had two little boys, six and eight, who lived with their mother outside Los Angeles. He sighed and gave a sad smile. Now he'd get to see them more. He was finishing a book on how the mind works and had a publisher lined up. I told him I had also taken time off work, was recently divorced, came to the Zen Center regularly and lived by the bay.

We were quiet for a moment, then he said in a tentative tone, "I'm renting an apartment near Balboa Park. Would you like to get together for a walk sometime?"

He might as well have pulled the lever on a fire alarm. I heard a bleating siren and saw *Date! Date! Date!* flashing red in my mind.

My throat closed up.

"I'm not interested in going out. That's not why I'm here." My voice was brittle. "Excuse me. I've got to go. I promised to create a bouquet for the Center."

I jumped up, wiped my hands on my overalls and darted down the hill.

My degree of panic surprised me. Aside from one miserable blind date a friend had talked me into, I hadn't gone out since Lee had left. I fully expected to start dating again, just not quite yet. Besides, I'd never imagined I'd have to contend with someone coming on to me here. This was the Zen Center, not some pick-up bar. It had always been a safe place.

I plodded down the hill and darted around some shrubs. There wasn't much to harvest for a bouquet. Eventually I cut off some anise, poppies and dandelions. I arranged the blooms as best I could, surrounding them with thin, dead weeds for volume and ragweed for color. It looked like crap.

I'd set the bouquet nearby on the ground and was already back in the garden ripping out more weeds when David strolled by. He looked at my arrangement and shook his head. "Not much, is it?" he said and snickered.

*Okay.* I understood his sarcasm. I'd turned him down and must have hurt his feelings. Now I glanced up and said in what I hoped was a friendly, neutral zone, "You said you were on sabbatical. So you're not teaching any courses this year."

"That's what the word 'sabbatical' means," he said, his voice clipped and cold.

I stared at him defiantly. *Jerk.* He glared back and turned away.

The last time I saw David that day, he was standing by a folding table, holding a cup of tea and leaning toward a woman I recognized but didn't know. She had wide hips and no chin. She was nodding encouragingly at him.

I thought about David over the next week. He was educated, accomplished, verbal. He wasn't an athlete. In fact, he didn't look like he worked out at all. This was just the kind of man I'd avoided, one who would challenge me mentally, not physically.

I'd hated dating, with all its passivity, flirtation and uncertainty, and was terrible at it. But if I was ever going to create a good relationship, I had to improve my skills. Then an idea came to me—I would ask David out for practice.

I didn't know his last name but the psychology department secretary at the university did because there was only one professor there on sabbatical: Taylor. So far, so good. I flipped open the phone book. There were twelve David Taylors in the San Diego edition and ten of them lived reasonably close to Balboa Park. Even this problem was surmountable. I'd go down the list until I found the right one.

I didn't want to sound nervous, so I prepared a short script. "Hello. I don't know if you remember me. We met at the Zen Center last week. My name is Nina. I'm wondering if you would like to get together for dinner on Saturday."

The first David Taylor wasn't home. The second was and he hesitated, then gave a warm rich laugh, saying of course he remembered me. His voice was so much more confident and happier than I recalled that he didn't sound like the same man. He said he'd love to go out and, in fact, he was getting together with a group of friends from the university midweek to see a movie, *The Attack of the Killer Tomatoes*. Would I like to come along? I couldn't. I was busy.

We arranged to meet at my apartment on Saturday.

David had only seen me in baggy overalls and work-boots. I wanted to look attractive for the date. After trying numerous combinations from my wardrobe, I finally put together what I thought was a knockout outfit consisting of pieces I'd owned but never wore together: tight black pants, a black silk blouse, a fitted black suit jacket, espadrille sandals with two-inch heels and a Panama fedora hat. Rather than wearing jewelry, I buttoned the blouse up to the collar and added a slender vintage black tie I'd found at a thrift shop. I'd never worn a tie but, suddenly, donning it seemed inspired. When I faced the mirror, the woman looking back bore little resemblance to me. She appeared six inches taller, willowy, intriguing.

I was almost certain that the outfit was perfect, but just to be sure I called my friend Carrie and asked her to come over for a second opinion. Carrie and I had been in graduate school together. She looked like a cheerleader with a pert little nose, a dash of freckles and cornflower-blue eyes. She was the only woman I knew who thought flirting was fun.

"What do you think?" I said when she walked in. I stepped back in my all-black ensemble and turned around slowly.

"It's amazing," she said. "It makes you look tall. Thin. Like a model."

I nodded, excited.

She continued to stare at me.

"It's just perfect." She paused and grinned. "All that's

missing is a gun."

Oh God! I'd created a gangster costume. How had I missed it? I'd layered myself in armor that said "look but don't touch."

Carrie strode over to my closet and evaluated everything on a hanger, finally settling on a pair of ordinary blue cotton pants and a collarless, loose-fitting, white silk blouse.

"That's more like it," she said, when I put them on. She tapped a spot between her breasts. "Now open the top button." I did. She tilted her head to the side, studying me, then commanded, "And the next."

I slowly unfastened it, glancing down to see how bad it was.

Carrie nodded. "Okay. Remember. Just like that."

"I feel uncomfortable. Exposed."

She gave a little shrug. "You asked for my advice. Trust me. This is how you want to look on a date."

# 35

E ven though I'd already met David once, I wouldn't have known him when I opened the door. He wore a burnt sienna colored shirt, rolled up at the elbows, unbuttoned low enough to reveal a hint of curly dark hair. His brown eyes were amused, intelligent, seeking, the gaze of someone engaged by life. He didn't seem to be wearing any cologne but he smelled like fresh ground almonds and bittersweet chocolate—a fragrance so personal, so enveloping, it confused me.

"Do you want to come in before we head to the restaurant?" I said, stepping aside, surprised at how unsteady I felt.

His eyes flashed as he glanced at me in my Carrie-inspired outfit. And when he followed me into my home, his mouth opened in a look of wonder. I had planned on decorating my apartment in a spartan, Zen style, but when I began arranging my possessions, someone else seemed to be in charge, a woman much more sensuous than I'd ever been. Plants hung from the ceiling and lined the corners of the room, lush and leafy. Silk Japanese obis colored the walls. Throw pillows lay across the couch and encircled the low dining room table.

"This is amazing," David said as he slowly paced the room, his voice comforting, like a shawl across my back.

We walked to a restaurant a few blocks away and over dinner we talked about our lives. He was thirty-seven, five years my senior, older and much more interesting than any man I'd ever dated. Later, when we'd finished eating, I suggested we take a longer route back to my apartment and stroll by the bay. There, he wrapped me in his arms and kissed me with a sensuality and confidence I'd never felt. David was someone I'd asked out for practice but now all I could think was *Holy shit. I am in big trouble. This is a man and I've been messing with boys.*

By our next date, I knew I'd marry David. If anyone had asked me if love at first sight was possible, I'd have assured them no one gets swept away like that. But here it was, the very thing or something close to it, love at second sight. Just before the evening ended—after another dinner out and discussing plans to see each other soon—I stepped in close, stood toe-to-toe with David, looked up and asked, "Where do you think this relationship is going?"

He grinned at me before glancing away. "I think I know, but I'm not ready to say yet."

After that, for the next dozen dates or so, something strange happened to me. I was too jittery to look at him when I opened the door. I felt like a thirteen-year-old at her first cotillion, but not the cool, in-charge teenager I'd been at that age—someone else altogether—an innocent. I'd duck my head down when he entered and mutter, "I'm sorry. I can't look at you yet." Then I'd skitter around the room, unable to sit or stand still, like a hummingbird trapped indoors. Sometimes, I'd catch glimpses of David watching me, a look of tenderness and amusement on his face. He proposed different things to help me feel at ease at the outset of each evening: wine, deep breathing, meditation. We tried them all on successive dates and eventually I'd be able to meet his eyes. But nothing held. I'd be just as fluttery and agitated the next time I saw him. This went on for over a month and, although I felt embarrassed, the emergence of a stammering adolescent also delighted me. I'd never allowed myself to feel so out of control.

# 36

We would rather have stayed in warm San Diego but since neither of us had work in Southern California, I accompanied David back to upstate New York after his sabbatical ended. I got a job writing promotional materials in the marketing department of a big hospital. Two years later, surrounded by twenty-five friends, we were married. It had taken us that long because—even though we'd never dated anyone else, even though I'd worn David's engagement ring and we'd been living together—we both feared another failed marriage. When we finally agreed to hurl ourselves into matrimony, we set the date just a month out so we'd be less inclined to back out. Still, we began bickering more and more as the day drew close, so much so that the Unitarian minister we'd picked for the ceremony gently suggested we consider other options. She said some people were better off cohabiting.

Our wedding was held on a vibrant spring day, the kind of weather that would have been perfect for an outdoor ceremony. But since we were in upstate New York, where rainstorms rolled in fast and unpredictably, we'd opted to hold the event at Susan B. Anthony Hall, a large room the Unitarians had designed for lectures, not weddings. Still, it felt like the right location. The name of the hall alone, honoring the great Rochester-born suffrage leader, appealed to the feminist in me. Plus, the hall had been available on short notice and was cheap.

It hadn't made sense to buy special wedding clothes. Professors rarely needed suits but David had one, which he wore, a gold corduroy with wide ribs and big lapels in a style that had been popular ten years earlier. I'd bought a polyester cocktail dress, cream-colored with purple trim, at a local clothing store, a simple outfit I knew I could wear later. But I did end up with one festive touch. It was lilac season in Rochester and the hairdresser who styled my pageboy that morning snatched a few fragrant blooms from the vase on his station and fastened them over my ear.

David and I had written our own ceremony during afternoon walks in the woods but we'd never rehearsed. We hadn't realized the real burden would fall on the minister, who was called on to hold the script, two lit candles and a cup of water all at the same time. Watching her attempt the juggling act during the ceremony, I thought I'd lose all composure and start laughing. But when she made it through, my relief was tremendous. All that remained was our celebration. My mother had driven up from Long Island with Alvin, her new husband, the man I'd met in the Manhattan restaurant. She was treating us to a wedding reception at Chez Suzanne Café, a small French restaurant opening that afternoon just for our party.

We deliberately hadn't ordered a wedding cake. David and I selected the chocolate mousse cake, one of the restaurant's standard desserts: no tiers, no swirls, no brittle plastic bride and groom mired in frosting. But the owner of the restaurant had other plans. He wheeled out a draped cart holding a large layer cake decorated with elaborate icing flourishes. Real white rose petals were scattered at the base. He stopped in the opening of the U-shaped arrangement of dining tables, turned to me and tilted his head, one eyebrow up: Was I pleased? I nodded, surprised. It was kind of him. The cake was lovely, much more costly than what we'd paid for and clearly his gift to us. He lifted the large silver knife on the corner of the cart and carved the dessert into slices. Then he pivoted on his heel, straight-backed as a soldier, a look of pleasure on his face, and exited toward the kitchen.

Our guests started chanting, "Cake. Cake. Cake."

Several couples, David's friends from the university, banged their forks on the table. A few people pounded their fists. Water glasses shook. They seemed almost angry.

"Come on. Let's do it," David said, touching my shoulder and pointing to the front of the room.

He rose and started walking. But when I tried to stand, everything swayed: the room, my vision, my stomach. All day, I'd been too nervous to eat but I'd joined in every toast. The champagne hadn't tasted like alcohol at all, more like apple cider. I wasn't sure, but I thought I must have downed at least five glasses, much more than I'd ever drunk.

The best toast had been the last, David's, only minutes before. He'd stood, made a show of glancing at his watch, then said, "Well, I've been married about half an hour now and so far, it's going very well." Everyone laughed.

I managed to stand on my second try, setting each foot down carefully to keep my balance. I edged past the lively secretary from the marketing department and her husband, both still smacking the edge of the table and calling for cake. It seemed to take a long time to reach the front. David was already there, grinning, holding his hands up, an entertainer coming onstage for an encore.

I expected him to put a slice of cake on one of the plates, pick up a fork and feed me a bite. But instead he scooped up an entire piece in his hand. *Was this what we were supposed to do?* I glanced at David. His face appeared shiny under the lights, his beard wild. I looked around at our guests. Maggie, my boss, was nodding and smiling. My friend Beth from yoga class raised her champagne glass toward us.

Our guests shouted, "Cake. Cake. Cake."

I grabbed a slice in one hand, trying hard not to squish it. The frosting felt cool and damp, like mud.

David leaned toward me and opened his mouth. I could see his lower lip, but the upper one was hidden beneath a fringe of mustache. I opened my mouth wide, the way I did at the dentist's office. We crossed arms, like two swords in a crest, and slid our hands into each other's mouth.

David pushed the cake behind my teeth. It had a gummy texture that stuck to my tongue. Then he pulled his hand out.

I wanted to feed him the same way but I couldn't. He bit down on my fingers and trapped my hand.

*Was this supposed to be a love nip? This couldn't be right. He was hurting me.*

I started to pull back but he clamped his teeth tighter. I tried to wiggle my hand free but he clenched his jaw and began grinding his teeth back and forth. He was going to gnaw through my skin. He was biting down to the bone. My fingers were throbbing. I had to stop him.

I dropped my right foot behind me a few inches, just enough to center and set my weight. I rolled my free hand into a fist and cocked it by my waist. Then I punched my new husband in the sternum.

It was a special kind of strike, one I'd practiced on the heavy bag for years. At the last second, just as you made contact with the chest, the wrist set. This punch had only one use. It was designed to shock the diaphragm, shooting it into a contraction, forcing the air out of the lungs and momentarily incapacitating your opponent. It didn't inflict a long-term injury. You used it to gain advantage for retaliation or to buy time and run. But like so many strikes I'd practiced for a decade in karate, I'd never known if it would really do what it was supposed to.

David keeled over at the waist. The punch worked! I was elated.

Then I saw the faces of our wedding guests, staring open-mouthed. All motion and sound stopped, like a freeze-frame in a movie.

*I should have just cried out. Everything was ruined.*

David pulled in a deep breath and righted himself slowly. He brought his wrist up to his face with apparent effort and stared at his watch. He gazed around the room at our guests before speaking.

"Well, I've been married about forty-five minutes now." He paused, shook his head and sighed. "And I have to say"—he hesitated again—"it isn't going as well as I'd hoped."

The room filled with laughter.

Later, he explained that he'd clamped down on my fingers because he'd thought some cardboard had stuck to the cake, and he hadn't wanted to ruin the moment by spitting it out.

I looked over at the man standing there. David had saved us with his agility and humor, his intelligence and presence and most of all, his generosity.

I've never loved anyone more.

## AFTERWORD

I never planned on writing a memoir. But when I sat down at my keyboard to start what I'd imagined would be the first chapter in a novel, memoir was what came out. I wrote about the year my mother and I moved to Miami, when I was ten and we'd left everything behind. Even though I'd been writing for much of my life and earned a living using those skills, I didn't know anything about creative nonfiction. I started taking writing classes, going to conferences, studying books on craft and, for the first time, reading memoirs.

By the time I finished my draft two years later, I had learned a number of things, including a fair amount about technique and an appreciation of literary memoir. I also learned that the story I'd been working on wasn't the one I needed to tell. All the work on that draft had been a warm-up for the real narrative. The part of my life I needed to explore—the part I'd been hiding from, the story told here—was my own heart of darkness. It took me months to work up enough courage to start writing about the night I was attacked. And when I did, I sought help.

First, there were concrete things that had never made sense. The knife the stalker had used, for one. It was sharp on one side, serrated on the other. After I described it to my husband, David, he took me to a sporting goods store and showed me a rack of hunting knives. Suddenly there it was. It made me nauseous to look at them, but seeing the knives gave my memory form, made an image solid where there'd only been haze.

My mother and I had never spoken of the assault after it

happened. Not once. It took several visits to her home in Phoenix for us to find a way through our shared sorrow. I'd never realized how deeply she had been scarred as well. I'd also never known how guilty she felt, not until she surprised me by saying it had been her fault. She'd opened the windows in the den that night, coming into the room after I'd closed them, sure it was too hot to seal up the entire downstairs. Her confession stunned me. What had she done! Then I realized a stalker that persistent was bound to find a way to get to me. At least I said as much to my mother to help her feel better, although I wasn't sure it was true.

Gradually, I was able to feel my way back in time. After work, alone in my office, I locked the door, turned off the lights and sat at my keyboard, eyes closed, often rocking or crying, letting myself remember the sounds of that night, the smell of the attacker, the acrid taste in my mouth.

After I'd completed the first section of the manuscript, I thought the hard part was over. I was wrong. Early on, I'd been sure my story was a hero's tale, with me taking crazy risks, being tested along the way, but consistently becoming stronger until finally breaking free of old bonds. I saw my involvement in the women's movement, my years spent training in karate, as key parts. But when I wrote about them, the chapters felt flat. What I'd written was true, but tedious. I also discovered that my mother's presence in this story was largely irrelevant. At first, that didn't seem possible. She'd played a central role for much of my life. She was my antagonist, my ally and my muse. She was also a great character to write about because her personality was so distinctive. (The women in my writing groups loved the scenes in which she appeared.) But all these topics—the feminist movement, the martial arts, my mother—kept moving me further from the early chapters, so far away that I struggled to find the theme for my book. It wasn't until my editor, Diane Higgins Hannan, scrawled on a chapter she'd read "This is your Big Book of Men" that I realized what I had to do.

Suddenly, I wasn't telling a hero's story at all. I had to write myself as flawed, controlling, weak and lost. I had to admit the truth about what had happened with Stephen—a source of great shame—and allow myself to remember his sexuality and attraction. In writing about Lee, I needed to reveal details about our relationship that I'd hidden from everyone. The scenes with him couldn't just recount his passive manipulation and his explosive temper. They had to show my willing participation in our dance.

Before I began this story, I thought I knew myself well. I'd spent years in therapy. I'd dissected childhood dramas, kept journals, analyzed dreams. But when I started writing, I realized I didn't understand basic things about my life. I'd lived with Lee for years before we got married, knowing all along he was wrong for me. Why had I suddenly decided we had to wed? And after I'd coddled him for so long, what freed me to make demands? My father had largely disappeared from my life once my parents were divorced. It was only after I started work on the memoir, after I'd created careful timelines of major events to help me reconstruct the past, that I realized what a catalyst he'd been.

Memoir can encompass many things and one of them is mystery. Ultimately, it was the mystery of my own life that pulled me in. But I first began studying memoir writing twelve years ago. That's a long time to solve one mystery and produce a single book. So, was it worth it?

When I tell people that I've written a memoir about healing flawed relationships with men, they often say "Do you feel better now?" as if the creative writing process were only a therapeutic exercise. That remark used to bother me because I want my work to be seen, first and foremost, as a literary endeavor. But the truth is, I do feel better. I'd kept much of this history locked away in a shuttered room. Now I've pulled back the drapes, opened the windows and let in some light.

# POSTSCRIPT

I never saw Lee after he drove off in early 1980, but I called him once, two years later. I was moving back east with David. Leaving California seemed so final that I felt Lee should know. He didn't seem surprised to hear from me. He said he was sure I'd call because he'd just dreamed about me. In the dream we were in bed together and I was asleep by his side. He looked down and studied my face, memorizing my features. He said the dream was so real, he felt he could touch me. There was a long pause; then we wished each other well and said goodby. But the conversation unnerved me. It also created a tug. I didn't tell David about the call until a week later and when I did, he was relieved. He said he'd known something was wrong because I'd been so withdrawn he was afraid I was seeing someone else. He asked if I wanted to go back to the Bay Area and see Lee one last time—to be certain. But I didn't have any doubts. Later, when I asked David if he really would have been comfortable with me making that trip, he replied, "Over my dead body."

Years after Stephen got out of jail, he worked as a bike messenger in San Francisco. I know that only because he showed up at the accounting firm where I worked as marketing director. He strolled up to the reception desk on the thirty-eighth floor with an envelope in his hand just as I stepped into the lobby to greet a designer who'd arrived for a meeting. Stephen had the same long hair in a ponytail, the same lanky frame, and the same style of denim jacket, but his skin was jaundiced and wizened. He looked like a Dorian Gray portrait version of the man I'd known. Even though it had been ten years since I'd seen him and I now looked corporate rather than hippie, I was afraid he'd glance over, recognize me and shout out something crude. It felt like a hideous scene from some soap opera. I ignored the designer, who'd just risen to greet me, and sprinted out of the lobby.

Paul and I have stayed friends. He lives half an hour from me and we see each other for lunch a few times a year.

My mother and Alvin were inseparable and stayed that way until her death three years ago. Alvin died last year.

David and I have been together for more than thirty years, moved across country and back, changed careers several times and continue to be in love.

## VISIT US ONLINE

If you would like to know more about the creation of *Grip: A Memoir of Fierce Attractions*, including cover designs that we considered, visit us at

**www.ninahamberg.com**

 NINA HAMBERG moved to San
Francisco from New York the summer
after "The Summer of Love." While *Grip* is her first book, she
has been writing all her life, both for pleasure and profit. Nina
studied creative writing at programs sponsored by Stanford
University, Duke University, and the Squaw Valley Writers
Community. She is working on her next book and lives with
her husband on the coast of northern California.

SEP 2011

CPSIA information can be obtained at www.ICGtesting.com
Printed in the USA
269668BV00001B/25/P